NATIONAL
GALLERY OF
ART
ACTIVITY
BOOK

25
ADVENTURES
WITH ART

# National Gallery of Art Activity Book

■ ■ ■ ■ ■ ■ ■ ■ ■ ■

## 25 Adventures with Art

Maura A. Clarkin

Harry N. Abrams, Inc.,
Publishers
In association with the
National Gallery
of Art,
Washington, D.C.

Editor: Robert Morton
Designer: Darilyn Lowe Carnes
Illustrator: Dolores Bego

All photographs in this book reproduce works from the National
Gallery of Art, Washington, D.C.

This publication was generously supported by a grant from
the Vira I. Heinz Endowment

Project director: Kathleen Walsh-Piper, head, department of teacher and school
programs in cooperation with the department of education publications,
education division, and the editor's office, National Gallery of Art

ISBN 0–8109–2595–8

Front cover: Henri Matisse. *Pianist and Checker Players.* 1924.
Alexander Calder. *La Vache.* 1970; and *Black Camel
with Blue Head and Red Tongue.* 1971

Back cover: A view of the East Building with Alexander Calder's
mobile *Untitled,* 1976

# Contents

Introduction  7

ADVENTURE NUMBER  1 — exploring shades and tints of color  11

ADVENTURE NUMBER  2 — what is a portrait?  14

ADVENTURE NUMBER  3 — capturing impressions of nature  18

ADVENTURE NUMBER  4 — sculpture that moves  22

ADVENTURE NUMBER  5 — learning about composition  26

ADVENTURE NUMBER  6 — testing the senses  30

ADVENTURE NUMBER  7 — "reading" a painting  34

ADVENTURE NUMBER  8 — finding a point of view  39

ADVENTURE NUMBER  9 — discovering patterns  43

ADVENTURE NUMBER 10 — keeping the balance  47

ADVENTURE NUMBER 11 — a painting with two stories  50

ADVENTURE NUMBER 12 — making art with action  54

ADVENTURE NUMBER 13 — the moods of the day  57

ADVENTURE NUMBER 14 — telling a story  60

ADVENTURE NUMBER 15 — feeling the textures  63

ADVENTURE NUMBER 16 — colors and feelings  67

ADVENTURE NUMBER 17 — shapes and motion  72

ADVENTURE NUMBER 18 — picturing the weather  76

ADVENTURE NUMBER 19 — what the sun tells  80

ADVENTURE NUMBER 20 — line, shape, and speed  84

ADVENTURE NUMBER 21 — learning about symbols  88

ADVENTURE NUMBER 22 — a face from the past  92

ADVENTURE NUMBER 23 — comparing old and new  96

ADVENTURE NUMBER 24 — creating a wide view  100

ADVENTURE NUMBER 25 — finding the third dimension  104

How to Visit a Museum  108

The Answers  109

Glossary  111

Picture Captions  112

# Introduction

This activity book is filled with works of art from the National Gallery of Art in Washington, D.C. Have you ever been there?

The National Gallery of Art is a special type of **MUSEUM**. A museum is a place where a collection of similar things is gathered, kept, cared for, and displayed. A collection of living animals, for example, is called a zoo. A building filled with rocks and fossils and dinosaur bones is a natural history museum.

The National Gallery of Art:

    GATHERS,

        KEEPS,

            TAKES CARE OF,

                AND DISPLAYS

works of Art that have been collected over the years.

Do you collect anything?

Where do you get the things for your collection?

How do you display your collection?

How do you take care of it?

The National Gallery has been collecting European and American art since its doors first opened in 1941. Today, two enormous buildings are filled with thousands of paintings, drawings, sculpture, and other kinds of art.

More than seven million visitors come every year to see, enjoy, and learn. The art is cared for so that hundreds of years from now people will still be able to come and see it.

In this book, you will zoom back in time and travel to faraway lands. You will meet famous people, witness exciting events, and come face to face with dragons and sharks. You will be an explorer in a jungle, a detective solving a mystery, and a person living more than a hundred years ago.

Claude Monet. (French, 1840–1926) *The Bridge at Argenteuil.* 1874

Antonio Rossellino. (Italian, 1427–1479) *The Young Saint John the Baptist.* About 1470

Peter Paul Rubens. (Flemish, 1577–1640) *Lion.* About 1614–15

There are looking games, trips of the imagination, word puzzles, and more. In all, there are **25 DIFFERENT ART ADVENTURES** for you to go on.

Here are some things you need to know about the book:

If you see a question followed by the symbol $\boxed{A}$, its answer can be found on the Answer Page in the back of the book.

Any words in **BOLD LETTERS** are defined in the Glossary in the back of the book.

Many of the art adventures have a special Magic Picture Frame: inside these Magic Picture Frames are answers to tricky questions, artists' painting secrets, and interesting facts about the artists and the art.

MAGIC PICTURE FRAME

# The Activities

All the adventures have activities that you can do.

Everyone can make art. As you do these projects, explore *your* unique talents. Do you have an eye for colors or shapes? Do you have a strong imagination? Maybe you are skilled at drawing something that looks very real; maybe you are better at making something that is very unreal. Be adventurous.

For many of the art projects, you will need basic supplies such as:

> crayons, paints, or markers
>
> plain paper
>
> construction paper
>
> cardboard or posterboard
>
> scissors
>
> glue

For a few of the activities, you will need some special materials—string, old magazines to cut up, feathers, noodles, and even flour and eggs. The materials and the instructions will always be listed. Some of the activities may be a bit tricky, so ask for help if you need it.

Take your time and enjoy all your adventures. You don't have to read them in order or do them all at once.

# ADVENTURE NUMBER 1

## Dr. Greenleaf's Tropical Discovery

You are Dr. Greenleaf, the world-famous explorer of tropical forests. You have been sent to this jungle to study the wild animals and plants. After hiking for miles and miles, you are very hot. You hope to find a cool stream. Suddenly, you hear water trickling. You cut your way through the plants and—SURPRISE! Animals are everywhere. They hear your footsteps and look up.

Henri Rousseau. (French, 1844–1910) *Tropical Forest with Monkeys.* 1910

How many animals are there?

What kind of animals do you see?

What noises are they making?

You look for the water that you heard, but it is hard to find. Wait. One of the monkeys is holding a fishing pole that leads to the water.

Why is the water difficult to find at first glance?

The water is green. In fact, almost everything else you can see is green. Plants of every shape and size are green, green, green.

Some plants are dark green, some are light green. How can that be? Look in the Magic Picture Frame.

## DARK AND LIGHT WITH BLACK AND WHITE

There are many different
**SHADES** and **TINTS** of every color.

A **SHADE** is a color with black added to it.
A **TINT** is a color with white added to it.

Where in the painting do you see the darkest **SHADE** of green?

Where in the painting do you see the lightest **TINT** of green?

Can you find at least one more dark **SHADE** of green? One more light **TINT** of green?

Does every color have many shades and tints? $\mathcal{A}$ 1

Look at the clothes you are wearing today. Are you wearing more than one shade or tint of a certain color? What color?

You must run back to camp now to write about your exciting discovery in your travel notebook. There are many different shades and tints of green.

The artist who created the jungle scene from these many tints and shades was Henri Rousseau, who was born in France in 1844 and lived until 1910. He was not trained to be an artist but decided to paint when he was a middle-aged man. His imagination and love of nature led him to create exotic jungle scenes filled with plants and animals that he saw in the zoos and gardens of Paris. Let his example encourage you to use your imagination as you try the activities in this book.

## Activity: Made in the Shade

What is your favorite color?

See how many tints and shades of it you can find, and create your own work of art.
Cut pieces from pictures in magazines, or use fabric scraps, markers, paints, or crayons.
Try to get as many tints and shades as you can.
Place all your tints and shades on a big piece of paper or poster-board.
See if you can make a picture or a design by arranging the pieces of tints and shades.
Be sure to give your work of art a name.

# Adventure Number 2

## Face to Face

Gilbert Stuart. (American, 1755–1828)
*George Washington*. About 1810–1815

Something tells me you're being watched.

How many eyes can you find looking at you on these two pages?

Thank goodness they are only paintings, not real people.

A painting of a person is called a **PORTRAIT**.

Gilbert Stuart. *John Adams*. About 1821

Gilbert Stuart. *Thomas Jefferson*. About 1821

Gilbert Stuart. *James Madison*. About 1821

Gilbert Stuart. *James Monroe*. About 1817

Today, an artist can paint a portrait by looking at a photograph of the person. But before the invention of the camera people having their portraits painted sometimes had to sit or stand still for many hours. (Of course, they took time out to rest.) They often had to do this for many days because it took the artist that long to paint the face, body, and clothing exactly right.

Sit down in front of a mirror and pose as if an artist were painting your portrait. See if you can keep perfectly still while you slowly count to 300. It's hard to do, isn't it? And that's only five minutes.

By looking at these portraits, you can learn a lot about the people who posed for them. You can learn when and how they lived and also make guesses about what kind of people they were.

How can you tell that they lived long ago and not now? Can you think of two ways? **A**₁

Why do they all have white hair? Were they all very old? Was it part of a costume for a play? Write your guess here: _____ **A**₂

Why do you think these people had their portraits painted? Keep in mind that there were no cameras in the early 1800s to record what people looked like. Because Americans wanted to have images of their leaders, presidents were in demand as important subjects for artists to paint. Thanks to artists like Gilbert Stuart, these men will be remembered for years to come—they are the first five presidents of the United States.

The big picture on page 14 is of George Washington, the very first president of the United States. Such an important leader deserved the best portrait painter possible. And Gilbert Stuart was the one.

During his career, Stuart painted three major portraits of Washington. The paintings were so popular that he and other artists made many copies of them. One of these paintings was the source for the **ENGRAVING** that is **PRINTED** on the one dollar bill.

(Do you know what a print is and how one is made? Look up Answer **A**₃ of ADVENTURE NUMBER 2 in the back of the book.)

Compare the portrait in this book to the one on a dollar bill. How are the two portraits different?

Why do you think Gilbert Stuart made his portraits of George Washington so serious? The answer in the Magic Picture Frame might make YOU smile.

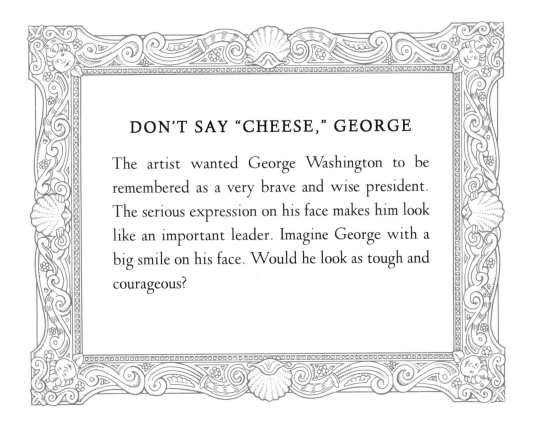

## DON'T SAY "CHEESE," GEORGE

The artist wanted George Washington to be remembered as a very brave and wise president. The serious expression on his face makes him look like an important leader. Imagine George with a big smile on his face. Would he look as tough and courageous?

## Activity: A Face You Can Trust

Now it's your turn to pretend that you are the President of the United States. The country wants your portrait to be on the new twenty-five dollar bill. Design the new bill on a piece of paper. Make it with any shapes, colors, and designs that you want. Leave room somewhere on the bill for a portrait of yourself, a **SELF-PORTRAIT**.

As the President, how do you want to be thought of and remembered? Serious? Happy? Fierce? Fun? (Try these different expressions in front of a mirror.) And what do you want to wear for this portrait? Do you want to be shown in a wig too? Draw your self-portrait, using the mirror to help, and think of the answers to all these questions.

# ADVENTURE NUMBER 3

## A Bit of a Blur

Try this experiment:

Find a table, chest of drawers, or desk that has many objects on top of it. Pick one of the objects—a pencil, coin, spoon, or ring—and look at it VERY carefully. Stare at it for thirty seconds.

Did you see it VERY clearly? Now turn away from it. What colors did it have?

Was it shiny or dull?

Did it look new or old?

Could you see any dust, scratches, or marks on it?

There are other things on the table top, too. Now, look at the object you chose again, very carefully. Can you see the other objects very clearly when you are focusing on your chosen object?

If the other objects seemed a bit blurry, don't think that your eyes are going bad. While you may have noticed their shape or color, you could not have possibly seen all the tiny details of every object at the same time. Why? The Magic Picture Frame will clear this up for you.

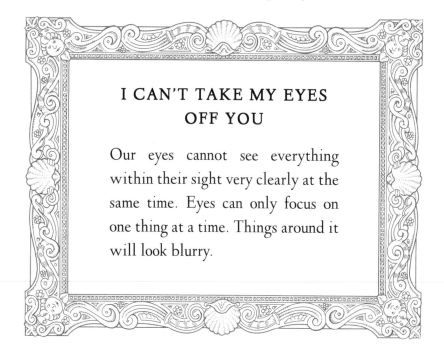

### I CAN'T TAKE MY EYES OFF YOU

Our eyes cannot see everything within their sight very clearly at the same time. Eyes can only focus on one thing at a time. Things around it will look blurry.

Auguste Renoir.
(French, 1841–1919)
*A Girl with a Watering Can.*
1876

A little more than a hundred years ago, a group of artists in France called the **IMPRESSIONISTS** experimented in their paintings with how they saw the world around them.

One famous Impressionist was Auguste Renoir who painted this picture of a young girl with a watering can. He painted a quick impression of the girl and her surroundings as they appeared at that particular moment in time.

Describe the girl's surroundings. Did Renoir paint in great detail every single blade of grass, flower petal, and pebble from the path? What hints did he give you instead?

What was the weather like? How can you tell?

Do you see parts of the garden or the girl that appear to have more sunlight shining on them? How did Renoir show sunlight with paint?

The type of brushstroke that Renoir applied in his painting was commonly used by Impressionists. The brushstrokes are (circle one):

short and thick        long and smooth

They look as if they were painted (circle one):

very quickly        very slowly

**If you visit the National Gallery of Art:** Be sure to look at other French artists, especially Claude Monet and Berthe Morisot, a woman artist who painted in a style similar to Renoir.

Claude Monet.
*Woman with a Parasol—Madame Monet and Her Son.*
1875

Berthe Morisot. (French, 1841–1895) *The Mother and Sister of the Artist.* 1869–70

## Activity: In Full Bloom

Now it's your chance to be an Impressionist artist. Picture in your mind a beautiful flower garden on a sunny spring day. What colors do you see? Using pastels, paints, crayons, or markers on a piece of white paper, make quick, short strokes that give the impression of leaves, flowers, and grass. Add lighter and brighter colors for the areas where the sunlight is strongest. Watch the garden bloom before your eyes.

# Adventure Number 4

## Hanging Around

In this picture, can you spot the largest work of art in the entire National Gallery of Art? It's not on a wall. It is hanging from the ceiling.

This kind of art is called a **MOBILE**. Do you know what "mobile" means? **A**₁

Can you think of another word (or words) that has **"mobile"** in it?

Here are two different pictures of the mobile. Both of them show the mobile in the museum, just minutes apart. What has happened?

A mobile is a sculpture that moves. What do you think makes this mobile move?

Believe it or not, it's not a motor. Air moves it. Sometimes the mobile moves in one direction; sometimes it moves in the other. It all depends upon which way the air currents are flowing.

Alexander Calder. (American, 1898–1976) *Untitled.* 1976

Much planning and experimenting went into designing a mobile that could move freely and easily with the air despite its enormous size. Alexander Calder, the artist who invented mobiles, worked closely with technical assistants to design this one in the National Gallery of Art.

He chose as the best material for the mobile (circle one): **A**₂  Why?

stone          clay          colored paper          aluminum

He designed the shapes, chose how many there would be, and worked out their balance.

How many shapes are there? _____ Red shapes? _____ Black shapes? _____ Blue shapes? _____

How are the red shapes similar to each other? **A**₃

How are the black shapes similar to each other? **A**₄

Many of the shapes are fastened to the mobile at an angle so that air hits them as wind hits the sail of a boat. The air pushes them and moves the mobile. The different "arms" of the mobile are at different heights so the shapes do not hit each other when they move.

Do you think the mobile moves: quickly or slowly? **A**₅     Smoothly, or with bumpy movements? **A**₆

Alexander Calder. *Untitled.* 1976

Pretend you are looking up in the National Gallery of Art and see these giant shapes floating by? Do they remind you of:

    clouds in the sky?

    the planets in the solar system?

    the humpy back of a dinosaur?

What else do they remind you of?

Calder liked to make works of art that were fun to look at. He wanted his art to make people smile, imagine, and wonder.

Calder didn't give his mobile a title. He wanted people to use their imaginations and create titles of their own.

What title would you give it?

**If you visit the National Gallery of Art:**

Alexander Calder made many other works of art, including the Animobiles you see below. **Animobiles** is the name his wife gave to these small sculptures of animals with heads that really move. Visit the whole Calder zoo when it is next on view at the National Gallery of Art.

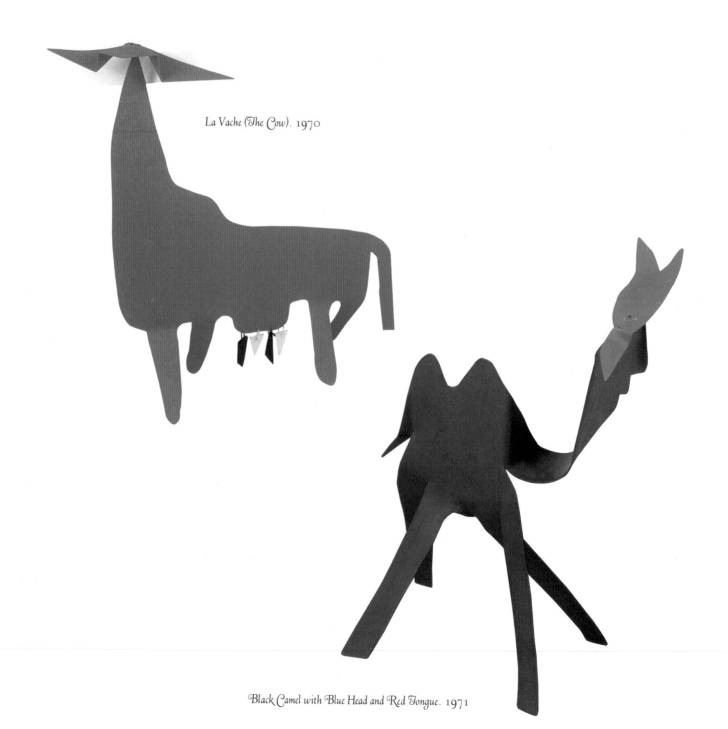

La Vache (The Cow). 1970

Black Camel with Blue Head and Red Tongue. 1971

# Activity: Blowing in the Wind

Make your own mobile. You will need:

1. two drinking straws or two straight, thin sticks about one foot long each.
2. string
3. construction paper
4. scissors
5. paper punch

Here's what to do:

1) Make a cross or an X with your two straws or sticks.

2) With someone's help, cut a piece of string about three feet long. Tie the straws or sticks together in the cross or X position, leaving enough string to hang the mobile when it is completed.

3) Cut out four shapes from the construction paper. They can be animals, letters from your name, or any shapes that you design.

4) Cut four other pieces of string, at least one foot long.

5) Punch a hole at the top of each shape. Push one end of each piece of string through the hole and tie a knot. Tie the other ends of the strings to the ends of the crossed straws or sticks.

6) Hang the mobile from the long string.

Experiment with the **BALANCE**, or the distribution of the weight, of the shapes in the mobile. Design different sizes of shapes. For some mobiles, maybe one end of each straw or stick can have two SMALLER shapes, hung on top of one another and connected by a piece of string. Make sure that these two equal the weight of the larger shape on the other end of the straw or stick (see illustration).

With other mobiles, the straws or sticks are not tied into four equal "arms." Two arms may be shorter and lighter than the other two. To be balanced, the construction paper shapes hanging from these shorter arms must be larger and heavier than the shapes on the longer arms (see illustration). Experiment to see what balances.

7) Try your mobile where there is a gentle breeze and watch it glide slowly in the air.

What title will you give your mobile?

# ADVENTURE NUMBER 5

## Angels and Angles

Look, up in the sky. Flying babies with wings. Do you think the French artist Nicolas Poussin really saw these angels with his own eyes back in 1626?

Certainly not. He painted the picture from a famous early Christian story about Mary, the mother of Jesus. Read about it in the Magic Picture Frame below:

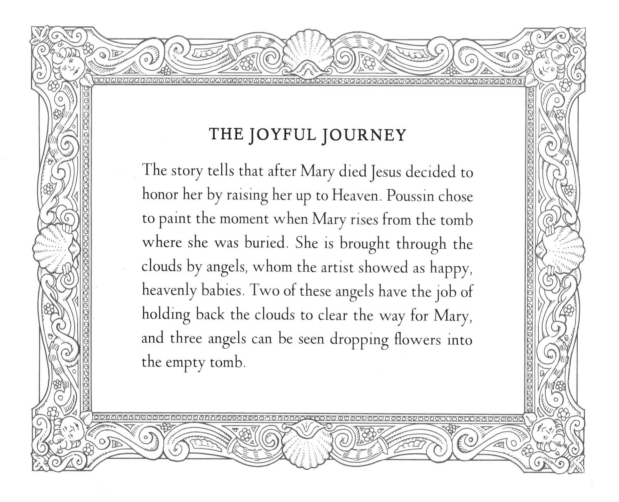

### THE JOYFUL JOURNEY

The story tells that after Mary died Jesus decided to honor her by raising her up to Heaven. Poussin chose to paint the moment when Mary rises from the tomb where she was buried. She is brought through the clouds by angels, whom the artist showed as happy, heavenly babies. Two of these angels have the job of holding back the clouds to clear the way for Mary, and three angels can be seen dropping flowers into the empty tomb.

That's a lot to include in one painting, isn't it? Poussin had to figure out how to put all the separate parts of the story together into one picture; he had to plan the **COMPOSITION**, the arrangement of things in a painting. "Where should Mary be placed? How many angels should there be? What should they look like and where should he paint them?" These are questions that Poussin asked.

Nicolas Poussin. (French, 1594–1665) *The Assumption of the Virgin.* 1626

A composition is a bit like a skeleton of the picture, the invisible structure that holds the picture together. Poussin's composition consists of simple shapes like **rectangles** ☐, **triangles** △, and **ovals** ◯.

　　Pretend that you can take an X-ray of this painting. Put a piece of thin paper over the reproduction on the previous page and trace with your pencil point the following shapes: **A**₁

1) one LARGE RECTANGLE made by the pillars (or columns) on each side of the painting, the tomb on the bottom, and the top of the picture.
2) one LARGE TRIANGLE made by the clouds.
3) one LARGE OVAL in the center of the painting made by Mary and the angels surrounding her.

　　While your eyes can't always see the composition of a painting, it is there just as a skeleton gives shape to a body, but is invisible.


## Activity: The Shape of Things to Come

From looking at the happy angel pointing upward and at Mary's joyful face, it seems as if Heaven is within their sight. What do you imagine that they see? Is it a giant castle that sparkles like diamonds? a large white gate inviting you in? a tropical island?

　　Use your imagination and make your own drawing or painting of your dream paradise. First, picture it in your mind. What do you see? Palm trees, huge white pillars, a throne, a mountain, or a rainbow?

　　Plan your picture by first sketching the composition or skeleton with light pencil marks on a piece of plain paper. Make simple, big shapes. Will the palm trees or pillars, for example, form the sides of a giant rectangle? Will a throne be a smaller rectangle in the center of the painting? Will a mountain be a triangle, or a rainbow be an arch? Try to have at least two different shapes in your composition. Then, add all the details of your dream paradise and color it in with crayons, paints, or markers.

**If you visit the National Gallery of Art:**

Use your special X-ray vision to see the compositions of such paintings as *Italian Comedians* by Antoine Watteau. Like Poussin's, Watteau's composition includes a big triangle. Can you find it?

Antoine Watteau. (French, 1684–1721) *Italian Comedians*. About 1720

# ADVENTURE NUMBER 6

## Come to Your Senses

Do you know what your five senses are? They are the five different ways you can experience things around you. See if you can name them here. One has been done for you. $A_1$

1. sight    2. _____    3. _____    4. _____    5. _____

Martin Johnson Heade. (American, 1819–1904) *Cattleya Orchid and Three Brazilian Hummingbirds.* 1871

Martin Johnson Heade, the American artist who painted this picture, paid very close attention to his senses. He liked to examine things carefully, to study their shapes, their colors, and their **TEXTURES,** the way that their surfaces looked and felt to the touch.

One of his favorite places to visit was South America because of its wonderful jungles filled with many different flowers and birds.

In this picture, he painted the flowers and birds of Brazil with such great detail that you feel as if you're in the jungle too.

And now it's your turn to be a good observer. The eighteen words below in **bold letters** are things that your senses would experience in this South American jungle. Answer each of the questions by looking at the painting and using your imagination. Then, find each word hidden in the word puzzle. THE FIRST LETTER OF EACH WORD IS TYPED IN BOLD SOMEWHERE IN THE PUZZLE. The words may be backward, upside down, or diagonal, so look carefully. Circle them when you find them.

SIGHT:

**orchid**—Do you think the petals are thick or thin?

**hummingbird**—What colors are these birds?

**nest**—What does it look like it is made of?

**eggs**—How many do you count?

**leaves**—Where do you see leaves?

**mist**—How do you know it is misty in the distance?

**branch**—Name two things resting on the branch.

SOUND:

**thunder**—Do you imagine it is loud or soft?

**rain**—Imagine a heavy rain storm. What will happen to the flower?

**hum**—Hummingbirds got their name because their wings move so quickly that they vibrate and make a "humming" sound. Try to make this sound with your mouth.

TOUCH:

**damp**—Imagine you are in the jungle. How would the dampness feel on your face?

**soft**—What might feel soft?

**stiff**—What might feel stiff?

**smooth**—What might feel smooth?

**rough**—What might feel rough?

SMELL:

**soil**—Have you ever planted a seed or played in the dirt? Soil has its own smell, especially after a rain. Imagine the smell now.

**sweetness**—What might smell sweet? Can you smell it?

TASTE:

**nectar**—Nectar is the sweet juice inside a flower that insects and birds like to drink. What foods or liquids do you like that are very sweet?

(puzzle on next page)

# The Puzzle

```
A  C  B  R  E  D  N  U  H  T  A  I  N  C  I  B  N  H  M
G  S  R  I  M  P  Q  B  C  S  I  C  A  V  B  R  P  O  R
F  M  I  S  T  D  G  X  M  D  U  P  R  C  T  K  J  N  L
L  O  B  M  P  A  F  G  A  K  C  E  G  H  J  M  R  P  S
M  O  A  S  X  P  V  M  W  S  W  Y  W  G  C  K  O  P  B
O  T  O  N  U  D  P  B  R  D  C  W  T  S  E  N  P  Y  M
O  H  Y  I  T  Q  Q  A  V  H  Z  O  X  A  B  F  A  Q  O
A  N  T  A  C  M  E  C  V  U  E  D  E  Y  O  X  N  R  L
T  Z  T  R  B  Y  C  Z  F  M  U  S  T  I  F  F  Z  G  B
V  U  B  A  S  R  B  P  D  M  C  S  D  B  N  M  N  R  J
L  M  R  U  S  G  G  E  S  I  Z  F  Z  E  T  F  H  E  G
E  R  S  H  G  O  F  S  R  N  G  Y  H  L  M  S  A  S  D
B  V  T  G  X  U  E  H  P  G  Q  B  Z  U  Z  E  F  Q  H
R  Q  E  P  N  N  V  O  X  B  A  T  L  K  M  V  I  D  G
Q  L  W  I  T  H  I  Q  G  I  L  Y  V  S  G  A  P  I  U
M  N  L  E  F  R  K  W  M  R  N  M  K  O  U  E  J  B  O
M  J  E  M  O  R  C  H  I  D  L  J  X  I  C  L  H  H  R
A  W  O  K  S  L  I  K  J  S  J  W  M  L  K  I  A  J  B
S  M  J  K  V  W  N  A  S  S  O  M  X  Q  B  C  U  A  V
J  A  F  N  E  C  T  A  R  N  A  R  O  L  O  C  E  G  G
```

A completed puzzle is on the Answer Pages.

# Activity: Try to Make Sense of It

Challenge your friends with this game of the senses:

Gather different things around the house or outdoors, if possible, that you can smell, taste, touch, and hear. (Below are some good suggestions.)

| | | | | |
|---|---|---|---|---|
| peach | cinnamon | garlic | nickels | the sound of a potato chip being eaten |
| perfume | lemon | tin foil | flour | something furry        leaf        woven basket |
| honey | pinecone | feathers | sponge | celery        a ticking watch or clock |

the sound of a jar of peanut butter opening

Try to include the following:
Something as sweet to the taste as the nectar of the orchid
Something as fragrant to the smell as the orchid
Something as rough to the touch as the bark on the branches
Something as velvety to the touch as the flower petals
Something as damp to the touch as the mist.

Put everything in a big bag. Have your friends close their eyes and hand them one thing or demonstrate it for them (like the sound made from opening a jar of peanut butter). See if they can guess what it is by touching, smelling, listening to, and tasting (if it is meant to be eaten). Show them the picture of *Cattleya Orchid and Three Brazilian Hummingbirds*. Can they match the smell, taste, or feel of any of the objects you give them with something in the painting?

# Adventure Number 7

## Do Clothes Make the Man?

Jacques-Louis David. (French, 1784–1825)
*Napoleon in His Study.* 1812

Napoleon Bonaparte was the emperor of France in the early 1800s. Like many leaders at that time, he had his own palace. Great artists were asked to paint pictures of him. Napoleon's favorite artist, Jacques-Louis David, painted this **PORTRAIT** of the emperor in 1812. The portrait is full of clues about how important Napoleon was and how hard he worked. See if you can find these clues:

**Napoleon is wearing a uniform of a military leader.**

He wears gold fringed straps as part of his uniform.

They are called **epaulettes**. On what part of the body do epaulettes rest?_____

Napoleon wears this medal and two others to show how honored he was by the Empire.

This gold handle belongs to the sword which the artist included as a symbol of Napoleon's military greatness.

Although he is in his uniform, Napoleon looks a bit messy. His stockings are wrinkled, and he has unbuttoned cuffs and uncombed hair. Why would this be? Let's look at the clues:

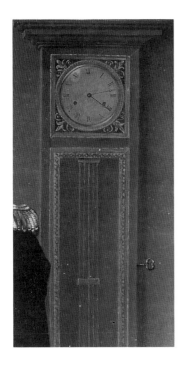

This clock shows that it is 13 minutes past 4 o'clock. Do you think that is in the afternoon or in the early morning? More clues are waiting for you.

These candles are lit. During which time of day would he need them lit, and why? Do you think they have been lit for a long or short time?

To solve the mystery, why does Napoleon look a bit messy and tired? **A** 1

Why was the emperor up so late? The artist provides the clues: On Napoleon's desk is the Napoleonic Code, a set of laws that he worked very hard to create.

Back in the early 1800s, many people, including Napoleon, wrote by dipping the sharpened, bony end of a feather in ink.

He's busy at work in his official study. The furniture and decorations also show us his importance and wealth.

The fabric on the side of the chair is decorated with golden bees, an emblem that signifies working hard and keeping "busy as a bee."

The wall decorations include these **symbols** from ancient Greece and Rome: the winged head of Mercury, god of wealth; and the eagle, symbol of power and victory.

Over 3,000 years ago in Egypt, beasts such as this were symbols of the power of the pharaohs (rulers).

Looking at all the decorations, we can guess that Napoleon wanted to identify himself with these different qualities of leadership from the past. He believed that he had those qualities too.

One last question: Why does Napoleon have his hand hiding or resting in his open vest? Did he have an itch? Did he eat too much for dinner? The Magic Picture Frame will bring the answer out of hiding.

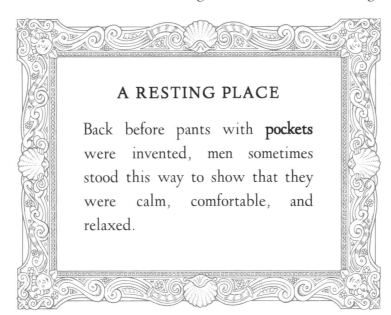

### A RESTING PLACE

Back before pants with **pockets** were invented, men sometimes stood this way to show that they were calm, comfortable, and relaxed.

**If you visit the National Gallery of Art:** See if you can find a portrait of a gentleman who is also resting his hand in his jacket. The portrait was painted in America in 1829.

Anonymous. (American 19th Century)
*Portrait of a Black Man.* Probably 1829

# Activity: A Real Winner.

As we have seen, the painting of Napoleon is full of clues about the emperor's job and his life. By looking at it closely, you can learn that he was important, that he had a military career, and that he was very hard-working.

Now it's your turn to show the importance of someone in a portrait. Pick a friend and pretend that he or she is running for school president. Your friend has asked you to paint the very best portrait possible, filled with clues about his or her personality, intelligence, interests, and hard work. The portrait should convince everyone that your friend will be the best president for the school.

Here are some ideas to think about before you draw, color, or paint the portrait:

Is your friend a good student? Include some school books or a report card for all to see.

What will your friend wear to look responsible, likable, and important?

Does your friend have the same interests as many other students, like sports or school clubs? Include clues about these in the portrait.

Has your friend won any awards or trophies that you will include?

In what room or space will you show your friend? A classroom? in front of the school? at a favorite hangout of the students?

# Adventure Number 8

## A Different Point of View

Do you like being the center of attention? Do you sometimes feel like a star, when everyone is looking at you and listening very carefully?

Look back at the painting of Napoleon. He certainly enjoyed being the center of attention. In the painting, he takes up most of the room and is right in the center.

Can you find another painting in this book in which someone is definitely the center of attention? Write the name of the painting here. _____

Edgar Degas.
(French, 1834–1917)
*Dancers at the Old Opera House.* About 1877

Now take a look at *Dancers at the Old Opera House* by Edgar Degas.
What did Degas place in the center of this painting?

Who or what takes up most of the room in the work of art? (Circle your answer).

the dancers                    the audience                    the stage

The stage: the artist has focused not on the people, but on the stage and the scene. Degas has captured the experience of watching the performance, focusing on a single moment in time. In another second, the scene will change and the dancers will move. In order to capture this moment so well, Degas spent a long time observing and sketching the scene and the dancers, recording their poses and movements. Then he created the scene from his sketches and his memory. What viewpoint did Degas create for you? Put a check next to the answer that you think is correct. $A_1$

_____on the side of the stage, out of the audience's view

_____in the first row of the audience

_____in the back row of the theater

Why do you think he chose this view to paint? Can you imagine what he saw beyond this frame, but chose not to paint?

Imagine that you were sitting in the first row of the audience for this dance performance. Would your view of the stage and the dancers have been different from the one in the painting? Try to picture how it would look from that angle.

Now imagine that you were sitting high up in the balcony in the back of the theater. What would your view of the performance be like from there?

In many of his works, Degas experimented with viewpoints. He believed that people and things could be looked at from all different angles, and that even the empty spaces around them could be interesting and beautiful to the eye.

**If you visit the National Gallery of Art:**

In *Boulevard des Italiens, Morning, Sunlight* (1887), French artist Camille Pissarro shows a city street with carriages and people rushing here and there. Where do you think Pissarro was sitting to see the street from the angle in the painting? **A** ₂

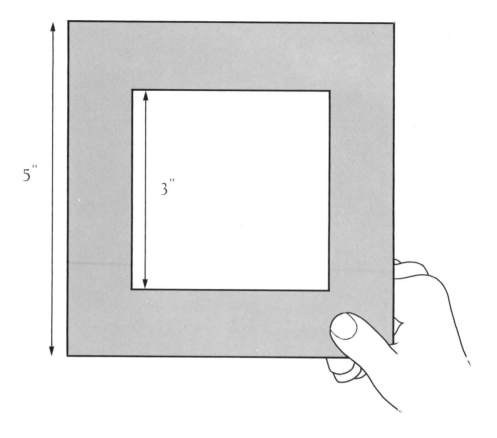

## Activity: Upside Down and All Around

Now it's your turn to see the world from all different viewpoints through your own viewfinder.

On a piece of plain cardboard draw a square five inches long on each side. Measure one inch inside this square all around and draw a smaller square about three inches long on each side. Cut out the small inside square, following the lines carefully. (You might want help with the measuring and cutting.) Now cut out the large square. You have a frame, or viewfinder. Hold it close to your face and look through it. What do you see? What things or people can you see easily? What can you only see a little part of?

Walk around the house or outdoors, looking through your frame at the world above you, below you, and around you. Do so until you find a picture through the frame that you think is interesting. Make sure that some things in your view are "cut off" by your frame so that you can only see parts of them.

Try to draw on a piece of paper what you saw through your frame. You can use markers, crayons, paint, or colored chalks, which are similar to the pastels that Degas enjoyed using.

# Adventure Number 9

ROW, ROW, ROW YOUR BOAT
Row, Row, Row Your Boat
Gently Down the Stream
Merrily, Merrily, Merrily, Merrily
Life is But a Dream

Welcome to Professor Polkadot's class. Today he is teaching you about **PATTERNS**.

Do you know what a **PATTERN** is?

A pattern is a design that is repeated over and over again.

For example, //////// is a pattern of slanted black lines that are the same size and the same distance apart.

Look at this pattern and cross out the face that is not part of the pattern.

Look at this pattern. Can you add three more shapes so that the pattern stays the same?

Are you wearing any patterns today?_____ What are they? Draw them if you can:

Professor Polkadot is giving you homework. He wants you to find a hidden pattern in the painting by Gustave Caillebotte on the next page. Caillebotte, a French artist from the late 1800s, painted scenes of people at work and at play. In these pictures, he often arranged the moving figures into a pattern.

Gustave Caillebotte. (French, 1848–1894) *Skiffs.* 1877.

In the painting *Skiffs*, three men are paddling down a river in France on a clear, sunny day. The pattern they form is a giant zigzag. Can you find it? To make it easier to see, connect the numbers in the drawing of the men paddling shown below.

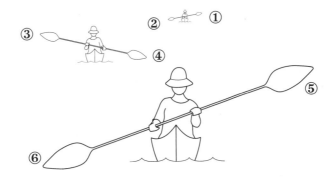

Why do you think the painter chose this pattern? The answer is in the Magic Picture Frame.

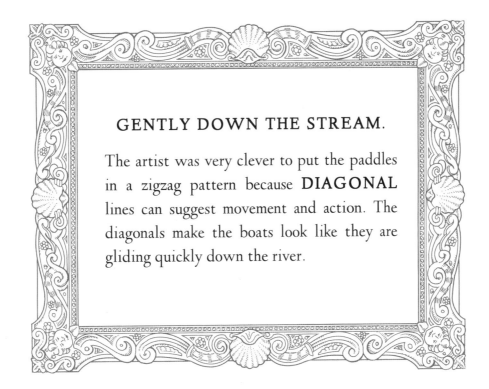

**GENTLY DOWN THE STREAM.**

The artist was very clever to put the paddles in a zigzag pattern because **DIAGONAL** lines can suggest movement and action. The diagonals make the boats look like they are gliding quickly down the river.

Patterns aren't always made of designs. Sometimes they can be made of words. Read the words to the song "Row, Row, Row Your Boat," at the beginning of this activity. In what two parts of the song do you see patterns of WORDS repeated over and over again? **A** 1

Congratulations. You have graduated from Professor Polkadot's class.

**If you visit the National Gallery of Art:** Be sure to see Henri Matisse's *Pianist and Checker Players* (1924), a painting of a room filled with patterns.

Henri Matisse. (French 1869–1954) *Pianist and Checker Players.* 1924

## Activity: Pick-a-Pattern

You may have never noticed before, but patterns are everywhere. Select one room in your house and see how many patterns you can find. Are there books in a row? Are there patterns on the wallpaper? On the furniture? What shapes, lines, and colors make each of these different patterns?

You can design your own pattern and use it to decorate writing paper, envelopes, book covers, wrapping paper, and more. All you will need are some markers, paints, or crayons and plain paper that is cut into the sizes and shapes that you want.

First, experiment on a piece of scrap paper with making patterns of different colors and shapes (for example, stars, triangles, flowers, zigzags). When you have created one that you like, plan how you will decorate each of the pieces of paper that you selected. Your pattern can decorate the top, bottom, corners, center, or entire surface of each sheet. Try decorating each piece of paper differently.

# Adventure Number 10

## The Balancing Act

If you have ever been on a seesaw or a teeter-totter, you know what **BALANCE** is. Each side must weigh about the same; one side cannot be too much heavier or lighter than the other.

Look at the three seesaws below. On each, a boy, who weighs eighty pounds, sits on one side. See if you can solve each math puzzle so that the seesaw balances:

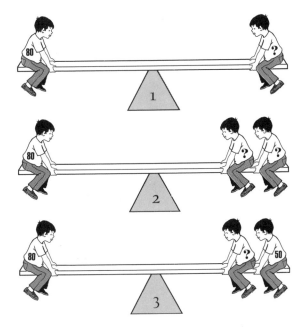

1) On the first seesaw, how much should the child on the other side weigh so it is perfectly balanced? **A**₁ _____ pounds.

2) On the second seesaw, two children who each weigh the same amount sit on the other side. How much should EACH of these two children weigh so it is perfectly balanced? **A**₂ _____ pounds each.

3) On the third seesaw, two children who do not weigh the same amount as each other sit on the other side. If one of these children weighs fifty pounds, how much should the other child weigh so that the seesaw is perfectly balanced? **A**₃ _____ pounds.

So you see, balance is an equal distribution of weight. Things on both sides do not have to be the same in number or in size.

Look at *My Gems* by William M. Harnett. It is a **STILL LIFE** painting, a picture of objects arranged on a table.

List four things the artist included in this still life:

1) _____    2) _____    3) _____    4) _____

Harnett was a master at balancing objects of all different sizes and shapes so that no one side of the still life looked too heavy or too light.

William M. Harnett. (American, 1848–1892) *My Gems.* 1888

Imagine drawing a line down the middle of the picture, dividing the painting into a left and right side. Is the weight of the left side and right side equally balanced? Look more closely:

The wooden table is divided exactly into two halves. What else is split into two by the imaginary line down the center? **A**₄

With your fingertips, cover the tall painted jug on the left side. How does that change the balance of the picture? Which side looks too heavy?

Now cover the books on the right side of the painting. Which side looks too heavy?

Cover other things in the painting and see what happens to the balance. Every single object plays an important part in this still life. Even the feather and the match sticks are needed to give the painting perfect balance.

## Activity: Keeping Your Balance

A **STILL LIFE**, as you know, is a picture of objects that have been gathered and arranged on a table top. Things that are often included in still lifes are flowers, bottles, fruit, and musical instruments because of their interesting shapes and colors. But anything can go into a still life, from shoes and spoons to playing cards and baseballs.

Now you can make a still life that has balance. You will need:
- —one plain piece of paper, any color
- —old magazines with lots of pictures
- —scissors
- —glue

Across your paper, draw a line that will serve as your table top. Cut out magazine pictures of the things that you want in your still life. For each object selected, pick another that will balance it. Are there some objects that you want to be in the center of your picture, much like the sheet music, pipe, and flute in *My Gems?*

Draw a line with a **light** pencil mark in the center of your paper from top to bottom. Then, glue on the pictures so that you are creating a balanced **COMPOSITION**. You can overlap pictures so it looks like some of the objects are in front of others on the table. This trick will give your still life a sense of **DEPTH**.

Keeping in mind where the center of the paper is, glue on the pictures so the objects look as if they are resting on the table. (You can overlap some of the pictures if you want.) Make sure you are creating a balanced **COMPOSITION** by placing objects of similar sizes, shapes, or colors on the left and right sides of the paper. You have just made what is called a **COLLAGE**.

# Adventure Number 11

## Tough Stuff

Most works of art in this book and in The National Gallery of Art were made to be looked at. Some, however, were made to be used.

Read the clue below to guess how this work of art was used originally.

"When I was painted more than five hundred years ago in Italy, I was not meant to be a painting to hang on the wall. I am made of leather stretched over a wooden frame. Although others similar to me were used for protection in battle, I was made to be carried in parades and in festivals before tournaments. At tournaments, knights in armor played a dangerous game on their horses called a joust."

Andrea del Castagno.
(Italian, 1417/1419–1457)
*The Youthful David.*
About 1450

WHAT AM I? _____

That's right. A SHIELD. Shields were first used to protect the body during a fight because, unlike some animals, people do not have a shell or natural protection.

What do turtles have for protection? $A_1$ _____

What do bulls have for protection? $A_2$ _____

What do skunks have for protection? $A_3$ _____

Why would a shield of this shape be good for protecting the body? $A_4$

By the time this one was made, shields were also used for reasons other than battle. They were carried by leaders during government or religious ceremonies as signs of status and achievement.

A shield made a person look important, brave, and strong. One sure way to look courageous and tough was to carry a shield with a picture of a powerful hero, creature, or god on it.

The hero on this shield is David, whose stories can be found in the Old Testament of the Bible. One of the best stories is about the battle between David and Goliath:

David was a simple shepherd boy serving as a soldier from Israel. His army entered a battle against another army that wanted control of the country. The leader was Goliath, a fierce and evil warrior more than eight feet tall. Goliath's size, however, proved to be no match for young David's quick thinking and skill. David gathered stones from the riverbed for his slingshot and, with one rock, hit Goliath so hard in the forehead that he fell to the ground. David took Goliath's sword and cut off his head, which he carried back to town as a sign of his victory, the triumph of good over evil. David's bravery and cleverness made him a hero. He became the king of Israel.

Look at the shield. How can you tell that David is a young, athletic warrior? Look at the way the artist painted his body, especially his right arm and legs. How can you tell he is in action?

Which part or parts of the battle did the artist choose to paint? (circle your answers):

Goliath leading his army

David with a slingshot

Goliath falling to the ground

The stone hitting Goliath

David finding the river stones

Goliath's head, after being cut off by David

The riverbed from which David gathered the stones

Goliath's head, after being hit with the stone

To understand why the artist made these choices, look inside the Magic Picture Frame:

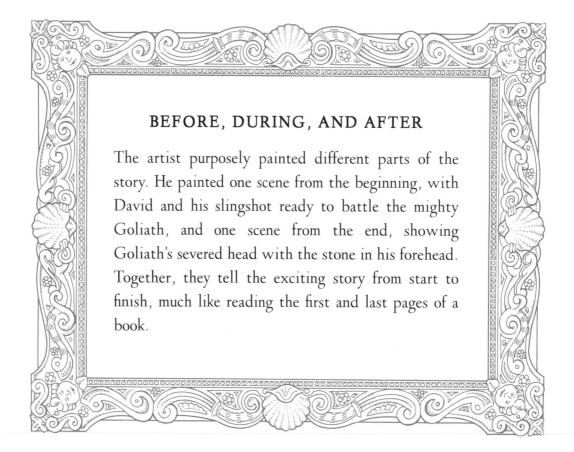

## BEFORE, DURING, AND AFTER

The artist purposely painted different parts of the story. He painted one scene from the beginning, with David and his slingshot ready to battle the mighty Goliath, and one scene from the end, showing Goliath's severed head with the stone in his forehead. Together, they tell the exciting story from start to finish, much like reading the first and last pages of a book.

# Activity: *Never Fear, Superhero Is Here.*

Make a shield with your favorite superhero or heroine performing a brave and dangerous act. You will need:

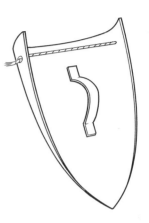

—a large piece of posterboard or cardboard
    (big enough to cover your chest and stomach)
—a hole punch
—markers, paints, or crayons
—string

Here's how:

1) Draw the outline of your shield on the poster board or cardboard. Look at the shape of *The Youthful David* shield for help. Remember that you want the top part to protect your chest and shoulders and, therefore, to be wider than the bottom.

2) In pencil draw your superhero or heroine in action. Make your picture big so that the body fills most of the shield. In addition to showing the superhero or heroine, can you show some of the story?

3) Color your drawing with crayons or paints.

4) Cut the shield out.

5) From a scrap of the leftover poster board or cardboard, cut a strip about 2 inches high and 10 inches long.

6) Bend this strip to make a handle. A view of the finished handle is shown in the drawing above.

7) Tape the two ends of the handle to the back of the shield in the middle.

8) Punch a hole at the two upper corners of the shield.

9) On the back side of the shield, tie a piece of string from one hole to another, just tightly enough that the shield arches a little bit. This rounded shape would protect your body if you were in battle.

How do you feel behind your shield with your superhero or heroine? Protected? Like a superhero or heroine yourself?

# Adventure Number 12

## Splish Splash

All the pictures in this book are of works of art at the National Gallery of Art. One of the difficult things about looking at these pictures in a book rather than at the Museum is that you can't tell how big the paintings really are. You also can't see very clearly how the artists made each painting; it is hard to tell if the paint is thin or thick or if you can see the brushstrokes of the paintbrush.

Look at this painting by the artist Jackson Pollock. Believe it or not, the painting in real life is much bigger than the size of some blackboards at your school. It is about seven feet high and ten feet long.

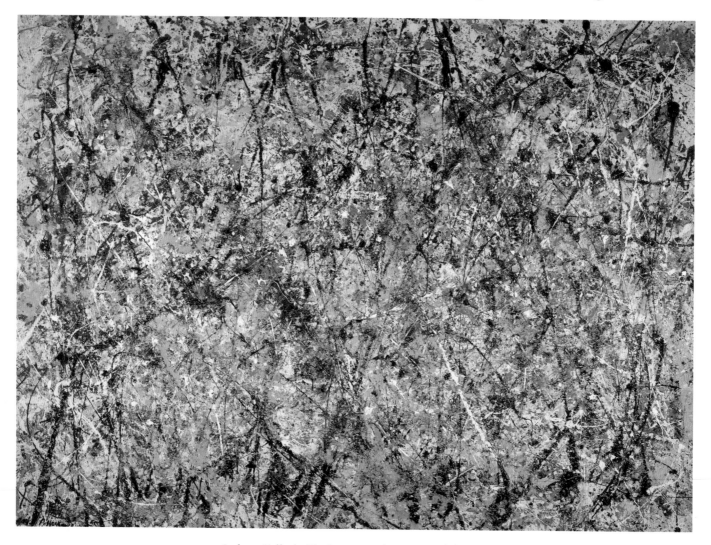

Jackson Pollock. *Number 1, 1950 (Lavender Mist).* 1950

From looking at the picture, how would you guess that the artist painted it? With one big paintbrush? With lots of skinny ones?

Now look at the painting close up. Can you tell better how the artist painted it? Look in the Magic Picture Frame to catch him in the act.

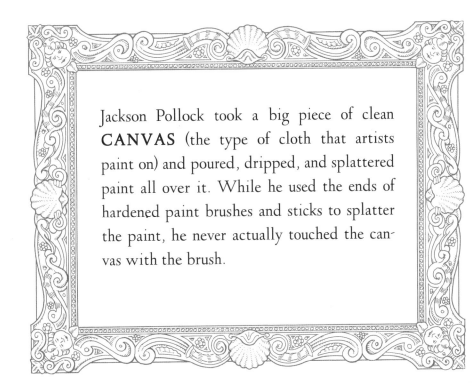

Jackson Pollock took a big piece of clean **CANVAS** (the type of cloth that artists paint on) and poured, dripped, and splattered paint all over it. While he used the ends of hardened paint brushes and sticks to splatter the paint, he never actually touched the canvas with the brush.

When the artist made this painting, he didn't put the canvas on a wall or **EASEL**. Instead, Pollock laid it on the floor. How do you think he reached all the corners?

How do you think he reached the center WITHOUT stepping on the canvas?

He walked around and around, splattering and dripping the paint as he moved. Sometimes he stretched or bent over to fling the paint onto the canvas. His whole body became involved in the act of painting. What colors did Pollock use? (Be sure to look carefully to find them all.) **A**₁

Do you think it took a long time or a short time to make? Why?

Do you think it was hard to make or easy? Why?

It may look as if it was done quickly and easily, but it was really a long and difficult project. Pollock spent hours and hours looking at the painting and planning his next move. He wanted all the colors to be spread out evenly on the canvas, so that our eyes wouldn't focus on one part. He also wanted to cover every inch of the painting so that none of the canvas would show through. This required thousands of splotches and string-like marks of paint.

Imagine if you were able to step into this painting and be inside it. What would it feel like?

cobwebs?        a dream?

outer space?        something else?

When a friend of the artist saw the painting, he said it looked like "lavender mist." Pollock decided to make this the title. If you have ever been outside on a misty day, can you understand why?

## Activity: Action

It's your turn to pour, drip, splatter, and experience the action of making a painting.

You will first need permission, because this activity requires special materials and can be a bit messy. You will need:

1) a large space where some splattered paint won't harm furniture or rugs or floors
2) a big, old smock to protect your clothes
3) layers of newspaper to protect the floor from the paint
4) a big sheet of white paper or butcher paper, at least three feet long, placed on top of the news-paper
5) tempera or poster paints
6) paint brushes or sticks

Start with one color and experiment with pouring, dripping, and splattering it from your paintbrush or stick. Move your whole body to reach all areas of the paper. Feel the movement of your hand, arm, and body. Enjoy the sensation. It might be fun to play music on the radio as you work.

Repeat the process with other colors until you feel that your painting is finished. Are the colors distributed evenly around the paper? What does your artwork remind you of? What title will you give it?

# Adventure Number 13

## It's a Mystery

Let's pretend that the Art Scrambler is a mysterious prankster who mixes up paintings and moves the labels that show their titles. All the Scrambler leaves behind are rhyming clues that include each painting's title and a short description of what it looks like. The challenge is to match the titles to the right pictures.

Recently, the Scrambler played the sneakiest trick, switching around three paintings by the French artist Claude Monet that are ALL of Waterloo Bridge in London. You, Detective Midnight, are the expert at solving art mysteries. You have been called in to unscramble this awful mess.

Look at the three paintings on the next page. How do they differ from one another?

The French artist Monet often painted in London, England, a city known for its foggy, fast-changing weather. He was very interested in how weather and the time of day made everything outdoors look different. The sky on a cloudy day looks different than it does on a sunny day. Sunlight in the morning looks different than it does in the late afternoon.

How does water look on a sunny, summer day?

How does water look on an overcast, winter day?

Monet painted at least forty-two pictures of the Waterloo Bridge, at different times of day and in different kinds of weather. The National Gallery of Art has three of them, and now they are scrambled.

Detective Midnight, here are the rhyming clues left by the evil Art Scrambler. By looking at the pictures and reading each clue, can you match each title and rhyme with the correct picture? Connect them by drawing a line with your pencil. *A*₁

*Waterloo Bridge, London, at Sunset*
Rosy calm,
Pink purple and sweet,
Reflections where sunshine
and water meet.

*Waterloo Bridge, London, at Dusk*
Purple and green,
Dusky dragon shades,
The water will darken
As the dim light fades.

*Waterloo Bridge, Gray Day*
Drizzly day,
Fog clouds and wind,
Wisps of gray
Float and spin.

MISSION ACCOMPLISHED.

# Activity: Sunrise, Sunset.

You can be an art scrambler for your friends and families. Cut from old magazines pictures of the outdoors that show different times of day and weather conditions. On separate pieces of paper, create and write titles for each picture such as "Early Morning," "Gray Afternoon in Fall," and "Summer Night." (You can also write poems like the Art Scrambler if you want.) Mix them up and ask your friends and family to match the titles (and poems) to the correct pictures.

# Adventure Number 14

## Shark.

It is coming after a young British sailor who is taking an early morning swim in the harbor of Havana, Cuba.

And what a shark it is. Can you see (check as you find each):

     _____ the shark's sharp teeth?
     _____ his mean eye?
     _____ his long, long tail?

Help is on the way. A boat, smaller in size than the angry shark, is arriving to save the boy. How many men are on board? _____

Can you see two different ways the men are trying to rescue the boy? What are they? **A**₁

1. _____

2. _____

How would you try to save the boy if you were on the boat?

Do you think the man with the boat hook will be able to stop the fierce shark in time? Yes _____
No _____

HOORAY. The boy in the water, fourteen-year-old Brook Watson, was saved in the nick of time and grew up to be an important merchant and a member of the government. But he did not want his story of danger, courage, and survival to be forgotten. He asked artist John Singleton Copley, an American working in London, to paint this picture as a record for history. Copley chose the most dramatic moment of the incident so it would catch people's attention. On the frame is a written inscription that tells the horrible story and states Watson's wish that this painting "might serve a most useful lesson to youth" about the risks of foolish behavior.

John Singleton Copley. (American, 1738–1815) *Watson and·the Shark.* 1778

**If you visit the National Gallery of Art:**

*Daniel in the Lions' Den* (about 1615) by Peter Paul Rubens is another painting in which the most dramatic moment of a story is shown. According to the Old Testament of the Bible, Daniel was thrown into a lion's den as punishment for disobeying the religious laws of a king. In this painting, a whole night has passed and the king, feeling guilty about his action, has just come to rescue Daniel. The stone that closes the den entrance has been rolled away and Daniel, saved from the lions by his faith, looks up and thanks God.

## Activity: Me? Scared? Never.

Think of a time in your life when you have been very brave in a frightening situation. Draw a frame on a piece of paper and sketch in the most exciting moment of your story. Where were you at the time? Was it day or night? Were you alone or with other people? What was challenging you? How did you react? On the borders of the frame, write a few sentences to tell people about your bravery, success, and the lesson that you learned.

# Adventure Number 15

## Ready or Not, Here I Come

James Jacques Tissot.
(French, 1836–1902)
*Hide and Seek.* About 1877

You have been invited to play hide and seek in the art studio of the French painter James Jacques Tissot. You and your new friends have just hidden around his big, crowded room.

**Ready or not, here I come** shouts the child whose turn it is to look.

**Oops.** Your friends have just peeked from their hiding spots to see if they are in danger of being found. How many friends are hiding?

You can't be found anywhere. You must have a wonderful hiding spot. Where is it?

The studio is a perfect place for hide and seek because it's so cluttered. There are chairs and rugs and tables and screens, each made of a different material and with a different design or pattern on its surface. Each has a different **TEXTURE**. Texture is the way an object's surface looks and feels—smooth, bumpy, soft, sticky, and so on.

Find all these different surfaces in the painting (check as you find each):

_____ paper _____ mirror _____ fur_____ hair _____carpet _____ribbon

_____ leather _____ glass _____ lace _____ wood _____china _____brass

Of the surfaces listed above, which ones have textures that are:

soft? _____        smooth? _____
fuzzy? _____        hard? _____

How did the artist paint the appearance of all those surfaces and textures? Three of his painting tricks are revealed in the Magic Picture Frame:

# FROM THE LOOKS OF IT

**Reflections:**

Sometimes when light hits shiny objects, a reflection can be seen. In a painting, a reflection is made with paint of a light color such as white. Can you find at least one object in this picture that the artist painted with a reflection?

**Outlines:**

Some objects, such as the blue and white china lamp, are hard to the touch. To show their hard surfaces, Tissot painted sharp, clear outlines. Other objects, like the brown fur in the painting, are much softer to the touch. The artist painted these surfaces with blurry, fuzzy outlines.

**Brushstrokes:**

The artist used paintbrushes of different sizes to create a variety of surfaces. The child's strands of hair, for example, were painted with a thin, delicate brush and stroke. Can you find something else in the picture that may have been painted with a thin paintbrush?

**If you visit the National Gallery of Art:** Be sure to visit *Fanny/Fingerpainting* by Chuck Close. She looks so real that you can almost feel every wrinkle on her face.

Chuck Close. (American, born 1940)
*Fanny/Fingerpainting.* 1985

## Activity: Shiny, Furry, Rough, and Blurry

With some simple material scraps and odds and ends at home, you can make a picture of a room that has REAL textures that you can touch and feel. You will need one piece of cardboard for the back of your picture and some glue for all the materials. Some suggestions for materials include:

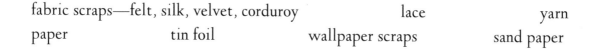

fabric scraps—felt, silk, velvet, corduroy          lace          yarn
paper                    tin foil              wallpaper scraps          sand paper

Use your imagination in creating the room. Will it have a carpet? wallpaper? mirrors made from tin foil? curtains made of lace or fabric on the windows? What material will your sofa and chairs be made from? Maybe there will even be old newspapers lying around the room.

# ADVENTURE NUMBER 16

## *There's More Than Meets the Eye.*

Have you ever watched clouds float by? They are all different funny shapes and sizes; no two are ever the same. But sometimes their shapes can remind you of things, like rabbits or dragons or fast racing cars.

What do these clouds remind you of? Use your imagination.

Many works of art that have been made in the past hundred years are like that too. They look just like designs with all their different shapes, colors, and lines. It is only with careful looking and your imagination that you can discover some hidden pictures.

Look at this painting by the Russian artist Wassily Kandinsky. He loved to make colorful designs.

Wassily Kandinsky. (Russian, 1866–1944) *Improvisation 31 (Sea Battle).* 1913

What colors did he use in this design? List six: **A** 1

1.          2.          3.          4.          5.          6.

Can you find (check as you find each):

a triangle? _____      a circle? _____      a square? _____      an egg shape or oval? _____

Can you see where the artist made (check as you find each):

a curvy line? _____      a skinny line? _____      a straight line? _____      a heavy, wide line? _____

Now take a really careful look at these colors, shapes, and lines. The artist has PAINTED A PICTURE WITHIN THIS DESIGN. Can you find it? (Hint: There are others that can be found in this book too. One was used by boys to fish in and another was used to help save a boy from a shark.)

What is it?

The artist has painted TWO BOATS in this design.

In this picture, however, the boats are at battle. Can you find (check as you find each):

a blue sail _____      cannons on the boat _____      a mast _____      a green ship _____
waves _____      a city falling in the distance _____

When you picture a battle in your mind, what colors do you think of? The same colors that Kandinsky used or different ones?

He actually chose these colors very carefully. He believed strongly that every color was like an emotion or a feeling; colors could be happy, angry, strong, or sad. So, in this painting, both the picture AND the colors express his feelings about the battle. You can learn the special meaning that Kandinsky gave to each color inside the Magic Picture Frame:

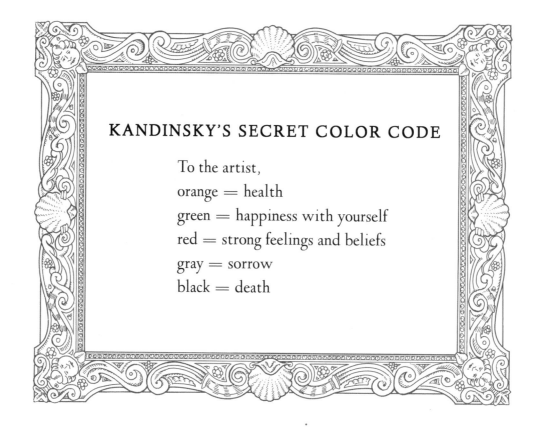

## KANDINSKY'S SECRET COLOR CODE

To the artist,
orange = health
green = happiness with yourself
red = strong feelings and beliefs
gray = sorrow
black = death

Kandinsky chose colors for this battle that he thought were both sad and happy, because while war and destruction are horrible, he believed that eventually people would bring about a new and better world.

Are there colors that make you feel happy? What are they?

What colors make you feel sad?

What colors look strong to you?

What colors look weak to you?

This painting teaches you that there is often more than meets the eye, particularly in art from the twentieth century.

**If you visit the National Gallery of Art:**

Be sure to find Pablo Picasso's *The Tragedy*. Picasso was an expert at using color to describe mood. And these people are certainly feeling blue.

Pablo Picasso. (Spanish 1881–1973) *The Tragedy*. 1903

## Activity: *Does Brown Make You Frown?*

Pick one of these emotions: happiness, fear, anger, excitement, or sadness. Think about a time in your life when you have experienced that feeling.

On a piece of paper, try to draw that situation. Where were you? Were you with other people? Did something happen? Next, decide what colors express to you that same emotion. Color your picture using only those colors.

Do both the colors and the actual picture communicate the feeling you want?

# ADVENTURE NUMBER 17

## Great Minds Think Alike

Think about a close friend for a minute. What is his or her name?

Do the two of you like to play the same games? Dress in similar clothes? Dance the same way? Act the same way?
You and your friend look to each other for new ideas.

Well, the same can be true for artists. An artist might like and admire the way another artist paints. Maybe it's the colors that the artist likes, or the way the brushstrokes look on the painting. There's something about the **STYLE, the way it is painted,** that the artist admires and wants to remember when painting his or her own work of art.

Look at the three paintings on the opposite page. All three were painted within fifty years of each other, between 1880 and 1923.

One of these paintings was painted by an artist who was good friends with Wassily Kandinsky, the painter of *Improvisation No. 31 (Sea Battle)* in Adventure Number 16.

Look at *Improvisation No. 31 (Sea Battle)* on page 68 carefully. Now look at the paintings opposite. Can you pick which artist was friends with Kandinsky and liked to paint in a similar painting **style**?

If you selected Lyonel Feininger, you are right. How could you tell that Kandinsky and Feininger liked each others' painting style? What is similar about their paintings? Answer true or false to the sentences below:
Both paintings are colorful

                    true                                        false


Both paintings look like designs at first glance.

                    true                                        false

Paul Cézanne. (French, 1839–1906) *House in Provence*. About 1880

Pablo Picasso. *Madame Picasso*. 1923

Lyonel Feininger. (American, 1871–1956) *The Bicycle Race*. 1912

Feininger's design includes two simple shapes that are repeated over and over again. Do you know what they are? Circle them here: **A**₁    ▭  △  ◯  ◯  ▭

But just as in Kandinsky's painting, these shapes also form a picture for you to find and see.
What picture do you see?

This painting is called *The Bicycle Race*. The triangles form the bodies of the bicycle racers and the frames of the bicycles. How many racers can you find? **A**₂

The circles form the wheels of the bicycles. How many wheels, or parts of wheels, can you find in the paintings? **A**₃

The artist's repetition of the same shapes over and over again made the racers look like they are zooming by on their bicycles.

## Activity: On the Move

How can you make a picture that REALLY zooms by? With a flip book. Have you ever seen one before? It's a small story book made only of drawings. There is one drawing on every page, each one "telling" a different part of the story. When the pages are flipped through quickly, the pictures actually seem to move. It's like watching a movie with a beginning, middle, and end.

Flip books are fun to make and use. Here's how:

You will need:     a pencil
                   thin markers
                   a small, unlined pad of stiff paper (about 4 by 6 inches)

1. Think of a simple story or event that you want to show in your flip book. Remember to make it have a beginning, middle, and end.
Ideas are:        a balloon blowing up and popping
                  a horse jumping over a fence
                  a car zooming down the street
                  a flower blooming—the example shown here

2. You will need to think of every single step in your story because a flip book needs to have a least 25 pages to work well. Every drawing must be slightly different, each one taking off from where the last one ended.

3. Start on the first sheet of paper in the pad. Draw your first drawing (you may want to sketch it in pencil and then use your markers) near the edge of the pad so it will be seen when the pages are flipped.

4. Turn to the page AFTER your first drawing and begin your second drawing. Look at your first drawing as a guide. There should only be a small difference between the two pictures.

5. Continue your drawings until your story is completed. Remember to always work in sequence on the pad of paper.

6. Make a cover for your flip book with a title and a picture. Now flip the pages from front to back and watch your story in action.

# ADVENTURE NUMBER 18

## How's the Weather?

Here are two different paintings by two different artists. The one below was painted in New York in 1902. The one on the opposite page was painted at about the same time in France. While they are both paintings of the outdoors, they are different in almost every other way.

Pretend you are the **weather reporter** for the day each artist has painted in his picture. It is your job to look carefully at each painting and decide what kind of day it is: foggy, breezy, cold, and so on. You must also report how people should dress and what activities would be fun to do. You can choose answers from the list below the weather chart or think of some on your own. Happy reporting.

Robert Henri.
(American, 1865–1929)
*Snow in New York.* 1902

|  | SEASONS | WEATHER | DRESS | ACTIVITIES |
|---|---|---|---|---|
| Henri<br>SNOW IN<br>NEW YORK |  |  |  |  |
| Derain<br>MOUNTAINS<br>AT COLLIOURE |  |  |  |  |

| SEASONS | WEATHER | | DRESS | ACTIVITIES |
|---|---|---|---|---|
| *Winter* | *Windy* | *Warm* | *Mittens* | *Pick flowers* |
| *Spring* | *Foggy* | *Breezy* | *Umbrella* | *Fly a kite* |
| *Summer* | *Sunny* | *Cool* | *Sunglasses* | *Drink cocoa* |
| *Fall* | *Freezing* | *Rainy* | *Boots* | *Go barefoot* |
|  | *Snowing* | *Cloudy* | *Sweater* | *Puddle-jump* |
|  | *Clear* | *Stormy* | *Raincoat* | *Take a nap* |
|  |  |  | *Bathing suit* | *Shovel snow* |
|  |  |  | *Shorts* | *Stay inside* |
|  |  |  |  | *Look at the clouds* |
|  |  |  |  | *Climb a mountain* |

Andre Derain.
(French,
1880–1954)
*Mountains at
Collioure.* 1905

Look at the activities you chose for each painting. For *Mountains at Collioure*, did you pick outdoor activities that are fun to do?

And for *Snow in New York*, are the activities quiet and cozy?

How did the artists create these different moods of excitement and calmness? On page 70, you learned that individual colors can make you feel happy, sad, angry, or nervous. But artists can also place colors together in special combinations to express other moods. The Magic Picture Frame will tell you more:

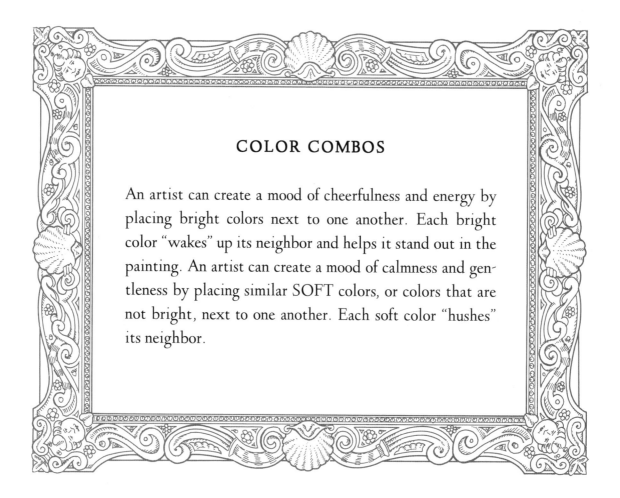

### COLOR COMBOS

An artist can create a mood of cheerfulness and energy by placing bright colors next to one another. Each bright color "wakes" up its neighbor and helps it stand out in the painting. An artist can create a mood of calmness and gentleness by placing similar SOFT colors, or colors that are not bright, next to one another. Each soft color "hushes" its neighbor.

What colors did the artist use in *Snow in New York*? Are they bright or soft? Are they similar to or different from each other?

What colors would there be in *Snow in New York* if the artist had shown a winter day so sunny that everyone would want to play outside? Try to picture it in your mind.

## Activity: Walking in a Winter Wonderland

Make your own snow scene of a sunny and clear winter day.

You will need: A piece of white paper

      Paints, markers, or crayons

      White craft materials: cotton,

       paper doilies, cotton swabs, and

       any white scraps you can find.

      Glue

On the plain piece of paper, glue the craft materials to create an outdoor winter scene. Cotton can be a blanket of snow, doilies can be snowflakes, and a row of cotton swabs can be a fence covered with snow. Be creative.

It will be color that will turn this snowy day into a gloomy or cheerful one. Look back at *Snow in New York* and see how Robert Henri painted in soft and dark colors to make a grey winter day. What colors will you use to make a snowy day that is happy and filled with energy? Maybe you can color in a gold sun, children bundled up in bright coats and hats, a clear blue sky, and evergreen trees. Make a snow scene such fun that you will want to jump in and make snow angels, catch snowflakes on your tongue, and go sledding down a great big hill.

# ADVENTURE NUMBER 19

## With the Wind at Our Backs

Winslow Homer. (American, 1836–1910) *Breezing Up (A Fair Wind).* 1876

Three boys and a skipper are sailing home after a long day of fishing.

Did they catch any fish? Look carefully.

Can you read the name of their fishing boat? What is it? **A**₁

Gloucester is the name of the town in Massachusetts where the skipper and the boys lived. It is also where Winslow Homer, the artist of this painting, spent a few summers painting more than one hundred years ago. He loved nature and enjoyed painting pictures of people in the outdoors.

Do you think nature would be easy or difficult to paint? Why?

One of the challenges of painting nature is that it doesn't stay still while the artist works. Clouds change their shapes, wind blows up water into ripples and makes waves, and the sun moves in the sky and bathes the earth in different colors.

Nature is certainly changing in this painting. A late-afternoon breeze has just swept across Gloucester Harbor.

Can you find at least three signs of a breeze in the painting? **A**$_2$

1. _____   2. _____   3. _____

Some clouds are also rolling in. Do you think the weather is going to change?

The sun is not visible in this painting. Do you think these storm clouds have covered it up or do you think it is in part of the sky that Homer did not include in this picture? Look and think carefully.

How did you decide upon your answer?

Can you spot at least three areas in the painting where sunlight is hitting? **A**$_3$

1. _____        2. _____        3. _____

Where do you see shadows? **A**$_4$

BONUS QUESTION: From looking at these areas of sunlight and shadow, can you determine where the sun is in the sky? (Hint: It helps to pretend that you are one of the boys in the boat.)

The sun is (select one): **A**$_5$
   A.  in the sky over the shore (where the boys are looking), shining toward them and their boat
   B.  in the sky to the left of the boat, shining through the sail and toward the boys
   C.  in the sky to the right of the boat, shining over the boys' heads and shoulders toward the sail

Not for long—a storm is on its way.

**If you visit the National Gallery of Art:** Be sure to see *The Mill* and other works by Dutch artist Rembrandt van Rijn. Rembrandt, as he is known today, was one of the greatest masters of light and shadow. It is not difficult in this painting to figure out from what direction the light is coming, is it?

Rembrandt van Rijn. (Dutch, 1606–1669) *The Mill*. About 1650

## Activity: If Shadows Are There—The Sun Is Where?

You can observe nature just like Winslow Homer. Go outside and notice the clouds and the breeze, the sun and the shadows.

Select one part of your outdoor view that has some areas in sunlight and some in shadow. By looking at those areas only, can you figure out where the sun is in the sky? Is it behind you? in front of you? directly above your head? (Can you feel the sun shining on your body? Are you casting a shadow?)

Next, make a colorful picture of this outdoor scene that includes these areas of sunlight and shadow. You will need to use different **SHADES** and **TINTS** of color, explained on page 12. Use tints for areas in sunlight, and shades for areas in shadow.

DO NOT include the sun itself in your picture; your areas of sunlight and shadow will be the clues to the sun's presence in the sky. Can your friends and family solve the mystery of its location?

# ADVENTURE NUMBER 20

## The Guessing Game

Have you ever played charades? Charades is a game in which you act out the name of a television show, song, book, or movie for your team to guess. You can't talk or use things in the room to help you. You can only use your body to act out the words.

For example, how would you act out a baby crying, a plane taking off, or an elephant walking?

Some artists in recent years play a game like charades with their art. Instead of just painting a picture of something that you can recognize, they think of a tricky, clever way of expressing it. You have to look carefully and guess what the artist was thinking.

The artist who made this work of art was thinking of a **sport**. Answer these questions below to help you guess which sport he had in mind.

1. What is this work of art made of? (circle one) ₁

metal          noodles          yarn          paper

2. If this work of art could make **sounds**, would it be **noisy** or **quiet**? _____

Why?

What sounds would it make?

3. If this work of art could **move**, would it move **quickly** or **slowly**? _____

Why?

4. Does this work of art look **safe** or **dangerous**? _____

Why?

5. Does this work of art look **calm** or **exciting**? _____

Why?

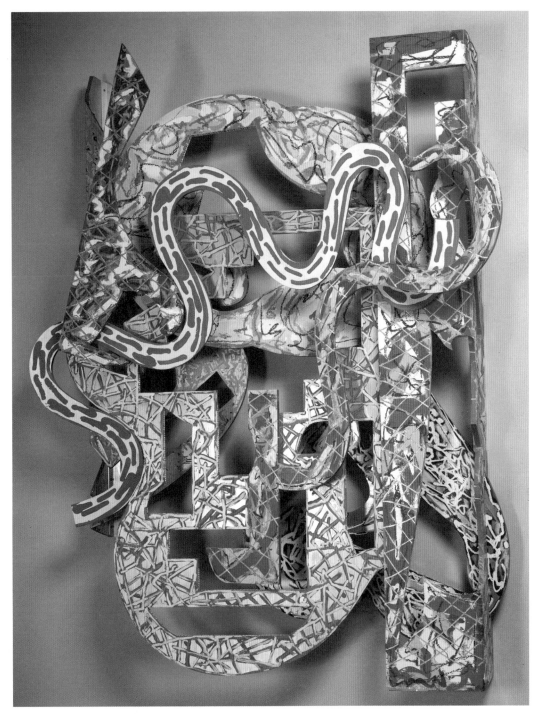

Frank Stella. (American, born 1936) *Jarama II.* 1982

Now look at your answers. The artist was thinking of a **sport** that uses **metal** and is **noisy, fast, dangerous,** and **exciting**. Any ideas yet?

For one final hint, look at the shapes.

Are they mostly curvy or straight? _____

Are they side by side or do they weave in and out of one another? _____

O.K. It's time to guess the sport. _____

To see if you're a winner, look in the Magic Picture Frame:

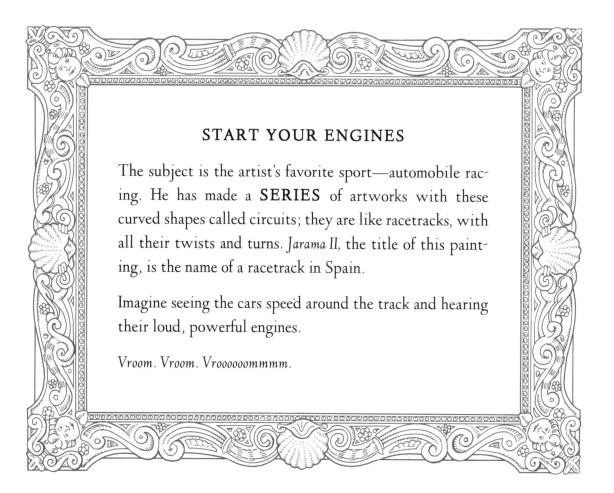

## START YOUR ENGINES

The subject is the artist's favorite sport—automobile racing. He has made a **SERIES** of artworks with these curved shapes called circuits; they are like racetracks, with all their twists and turns. *Jarama II*, the title of this painting, is the name of a racetrack in Spain.

Imagine seeing the cars speed around the track and hearing their loud, powerful engines.

*Vroom. Vroom. Vroooooommmm.*

Frank Stella created the idea and design for *Jarama II*, but he didn't make the actual work of art all by himself. He is a painter, and he did not have the training to cut the metal pieces and join them together; they were cut according to his designs by skilled metalworkers and craftspeople. Many artists work with other specialists.

Below are the different steps that were taken to make *Jarama II*. Can you put them in the order that they were done by the artist and his helpers? We did the first one for you by connecting the sentence to **A** 1.

**A** 1.                    Stella painted the metal shapes.

**A** 2.                    Stella thought of the idea.

**A** 3.                    Craftspeople put the shapes together according to Stella's drawings.

**A** 4.                    The metal was cut into shapes by metalworkers.

**A** 5.                    Stella made drawings of the idea and designed the shapes.

Have you and a friend ever worked together on a project or activity? Building a model, writing a report for school, putting together a play? Did you each have certain skills and talents that you used? Did you share the credit for the project when it was finished?

## Activity: In Bits and Pieces

You can make a work of art that will leave your friends guessing too.

Select an activity, such as bicycling, skiing, boxing, or dancing, and make a list of:

1) the objects or equipment used for this activity
2) the sounds of the activity
3) the movement or speed of the activity
4) the feelings you have when you watch or do this activity.
    Do you feel excited? scared? powerful? peaceful?

Think of how you can show all these things with just shapes, colors, and art materials such as paper and cardboard. Review how Frank Stella created the excitement, speed, and noise of a racetrack with curved shapes and bold colors. Make a plan and then create your mysterious work of art. Can your friends guess the activity?

# ADVENTURE NUMBER 21

## A Tiny Treasure

Rogier van der Weyden. (Netherlandish, 1399/1400–1464) *Saint George and the Dragon.* 1432–35

Here's a riddle for you to solve.

What covers miles and miles but is small enough to fit in the palm of your hand?
One answer is a map, but another is this painting, *Saint George and the Dragon*. Shown here in its actual size, it is one of the smallest paintings in the National Gallery of Art. But within this tiny space, the artist Roger van der Weyden skillfully painted a scene that takes you as far as your eyes can see. Let's look more closely.

The brave Saint George, dressed in his shiny armor, is rescuing a town and its beautiful princess from a terrible dragon.

See if you can find:

|  |  |  |
|---|---|---|
| a skull | the reflection of the town in the water | the horse's tongue |
| the dragon's teeth | Saint George's spurs | the dragon's scales |

If you think you are an especially good observer, see if you can spot these **hard-to-find** details.

two people on horseback
at least two ships
people walking up a hill
two trees with no leaves

Why do you think Rogier van der Weyden chose to paint such an important story so small? Its tiny size was proof of his tremendous talent. Its smallness also allowed individuals to view it privately and consider its meaning.

How did the artist paint with such brilliance and so carefully something which is SO small? He must have used a tiny, delicate paintbrush. Experts think he may have also used a magnifying glass to enlarge areas as he painted them.

Did Saint George and the dragon actually exist? Yes and no.

Saint George was a legendary warrior who is said to have lived in Asia Minor over 1,600 years ago.

The dragon, of course, never existed. The artist included him as a **SYMBOL**, a picture that stands for an idea. A ♥, for example, is a symbol for love. To Christians living 500 years ago, when this picture was painted, dragons were a symbol of evil. By killing the terrible beast, Saint George was really rescuing the townspeople from wickedness. The story was a popular one, and it was told to young people to inspire thoughts and prayers about leading a good life.

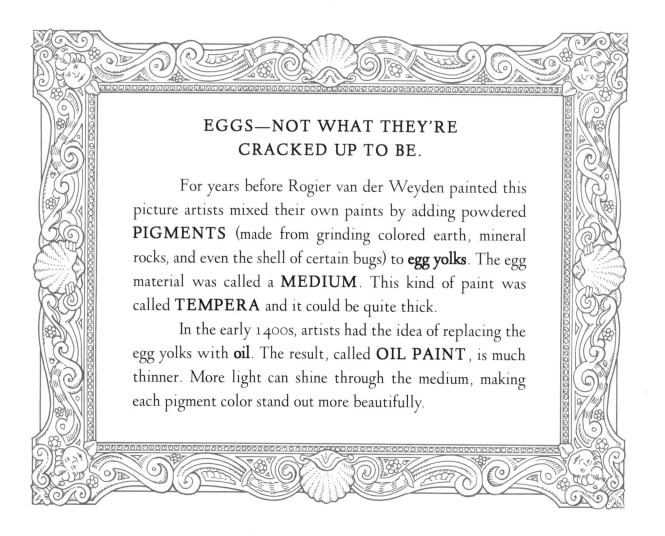

### EGGS—NOT WHAT THEY'RE CRACKED UP TO BE.

For years before Rogier van der Weyden painted this picture artists mixed their own paints by adding powdered **PIGMENTS** (made from grinding colored earth, mineral rocks, and even the shell of certain bugs) to **egg yolks**. The egg material was called a **MEDIUM**. This kind of paint was called **TEMPERA** and it could be quite thick.

In the early 1400s, artists had the idea of replacing the egg yolks with **oil**. The result, called **OIL PAINT**, is much thinner. More light can shine through the medium, making each pigment color stand out more beautifully.

With oil paints, Rogier van der Weyden was able to show the richness of the princess's gold embroidered robe, the shine of Saint George's armor, and the cluster of red roofs in the small town in the distance.

# Activity: Strong as an Ox

The dragon, as you just learned, is sometimes a symbol for evil. Over the centuries many other animals—both real and imaginary—have also become symbols for different ideas and qualities. Usually, the animals have been selected because they share those same qualities. Oxen, for instance, are known for being very powerful. As a result, the ox has become a common symbol for strength.

Can you match each animal on the left with its proper symbolic meaning on the right? **A** 1 The first has been done for you:

Dove          Faithfulness
Lion          Wisdom
Bee           Courage
Dog           Busyness
Owl           Peace

Now you can make a work of art with an animal symbol. Either select an animal from the list above, or create an animal symbol of your own. (Pick a quality such as gentleness, slyness, diligence or laziness. Is there an animal that is known for having that quality?)

Using paints, marker, or crayons, make a picture that uses your animal symbol to help tell a story. For example, a dove might fly above a city that is in great conflict. Or a lion might encourage someone who is afraid of trying something new.

Show your family and friends your finished artwork and teach them about symbols and how they can be used in art.

# ADVENTURE NUMBER 22

## My Name Is White Cloud

George Catlin. (American, 1796–1872) *The White Cloud, Head Chief of the Iowas.* 1844–45

As you're reading these words, imagine that the person in this painting comes to life. He stands straight and tall and looks at you with his dark, serious eyes. With great pride, he says slowly in a deep voice: I am **MU-HE-SHE-KAW** or **WHITE CLOUD**. I am the chief of my people, the Iowas. I want you to join my tribe and, with us, protect our land. Come, and we will give you an American Indian name, headdress, and costume.

Wow! Great! What should your name be?

### An American Indian Name:

Think of an activity that you like to do, such as running, swimming, skating, or drawing.

Then think of an animal that you like, such as a bear, lion, rabbit, or dog.

Put the two words together to make your name, like **Running Bear** or **Skating Dog**.

**Your new name is:** _____

### Face Painting:

Now you must have a marking on your face. I have a **GREEN HAND** painted on my mouth and cheeks, because I am good at hand-to-hand fighting.

Think about the first word in your new American Indian name. What could you paint on your cheek to show that you are good at that activity? If you're good at swimming, for example, a wave shape ≈ for water might be good. A foot would show that you are good at running.

Draw your face marking on a piece of paper.

### A Headdress and Costume:

On my head I wear a fur band topped with two eagle feathers and a deer tail dyed red. I wear long, pointed white earrings that were carved from shells. The wolf skin on my shoulders is covered with necklaces of bear claws and beads made from shells that are used for money, called wampum.

What type of American Indian headdress and jewelry do you want to wear? Instructions for making your own are in the activity below.

George Catlin, the artist, was not an American Indian. But ever since he had been a boy he had dreamed of going west to meet the American Indians and record the way they looked and lived. As an adult, he gave up being a lawyer and decided to follow his dream and become an artist. With his **EASEL** and paints strapped to his back, he headed west. This painting shows just one of many American Indians that he met along the way.

**If you visit the National Gallery of Art:** Be sure to see the other paintings by George Catlin, including the one below. That is one mean-looking buffalo.

George Catlin. *Buffalo Lancing in the Snow Drifts.* 1861–69

# Activity: Tribal Dress

Make your own jewelry and headdress with colored paper, fabric scraps, and craft materials at home. Here are two ideas:

1. Uncooked pasta of different shapes can be dyed and strung on string or wire to make necklaces and earrings. (If you want to use shell pasta or another kind that doesn't have a hole in it, soak it first, then make a hole to string it with, and let it dry.) Hang your "bead" earrings from two big loops of yarn that can fit around your ears.

2. Turn construction paper into a colorful American Indian headdress. Make feathers of different sizes and colors and attach them to a band that you decorate with a **PATTERN**.

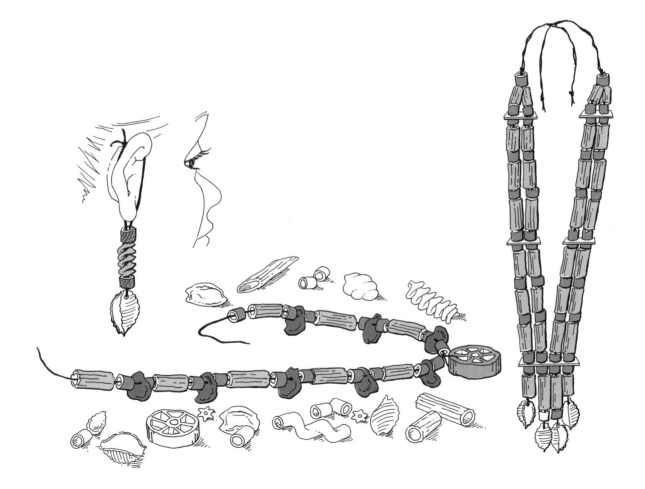

# Adventure Number 23

## Those Were the Days

A party. It's easy to see that people are celebrating in this painting. There is dancing, eating, music, and laughter.

BUT WAIT! Does this look like any party that you have been to? People are dressed oddly and nothing looks familiar. Why is that?

Jan Steen. (Dutch, 1625/1626–1679) *The Dancing Couple.* 1663

This picture shows another time and place. It was painted in Europe, in the Netherlands—the country we call Holland—over three hundred years ago. People dressed differently, ate different food, and lived in houses that were different from ours.

How do you think people traveled from town to town?
How do you think the men spent their days?
How do you think the women spent their days?
Where do you think they bought or got their food?
How do you think they cooked it?
How did they light their houses at night?
How did they keep warm in the winter?

Below, on the left, are small details from the painting. See if you can find them in the picture. They are of things that were very common 300 years ago in the Netherlands. On the right are things that we use today that have taken the place of the old things. Can you match the old with the new by drawing lines to connect them? 𝒜₁

Can you find a shirt collar from ANOTHER time in history somewhere in this activity book? Who is wearing it and when did this person live?

One thing that has stayed the same for hundreds and hundreds of years is that people like to have fun and laugh. One of the people enjoying the party is the artist himself; can you find his SELF-PORTRAIT somewhere in this painting, laughing with the people around him? **A** 2

**If you visit the National Gallery of Art:**
Throughout history, artists have painted pictures of where they came from and what life was like when they lived. These are just a few of many you can find in the National Gallery.

*The Card Players.* After Lucas van Leyden. About 1550–59

Linton Park. (American, 1826–1906)
*Flax Scutching Bee.* 1885

## Activity: What Will They Think of Next?

Look closely at the clothes in the painting and then compare them to what we wear today. If clothes have changed this much in 300 years, imagine what they will look like 300 years in the future. Design on paper an outfit of clothes that might be worn in the year 2300.

## Activity: A Taste of Yesteryear.

Below is a recipe that people made in Holland when this picture was painted in the 1600s. With someone to help you, try it at home. Boterkoek is a favorite Dutch cake. It's easy to make and delicious to eat—just follow the recipe below. First, check to make sure you have all the ingredients.

### BOTERKOEK (BUTTERCAKE)

½ cup margarine
½ cup butter
1 cup sugar
1 teaspoon almond or vanilla extract
1 egg, beaten
½ teaspoon baking powder
2 cups flour

1. Beat one egg in a small bowl. Mix together in a large bowl the margarine, butter, sugar, almond extract, and most of the egg. (Save a little of the egg to put on top of the cake.)

2. Add the baking powder and flour to the batter; mix well so that there are no lumps.

3. Place the batter into an 8 x 8 inch greased pan, press batter flat. With the back of a spoon, spread the rest of the egg on top of the batter.

4. Bake in an oven at 350 degrees about 30 minutes, or until edges are slightly brown.

# Adventure Number 24

## As Far as the Eye Can See

George Inness. (American, 1825–1894) *The Lackawanna Valley.* 1855

What does this painting have in common with Saint George and the Dragon on page 88?
In both of them, you can see the land for miles and miles around. But this picture is primarily a **LAND-SCAPE**, a picture of the outdoors.

This landscape shows the Pennsylvania countryside in 1855. The Delaware and Lackawanna Railroad had just been built. The president of the railroad, proud of his accomplishment, asked artist George Inness to paint a picture of the new tracks and buildings in their beautiful surroundings.

See if you can find these things that are near and far in the landscape (check them off as you find each):

_____ the church steeple in the town

_____ the tree stumps where the trees have been chopped down to make way for the railroad (The wood from these trees might have been used to fuel the trains.)

_____ the roundhouse where trains are stored and repaired

_____ the train traveling across the land (What sound would you hear as the train came closer and closer?)

_____ the boy resting on the hillside (What do you imagine he is thinking about?)

How long do you think it would take for the boy to walk to the roundhouse? _____

How did the artist show miles and miles of countryside in a painting that is small enough to hang on a wall? He used three special painting tricks that are as near as this Magic Picture Frame. Look inside.

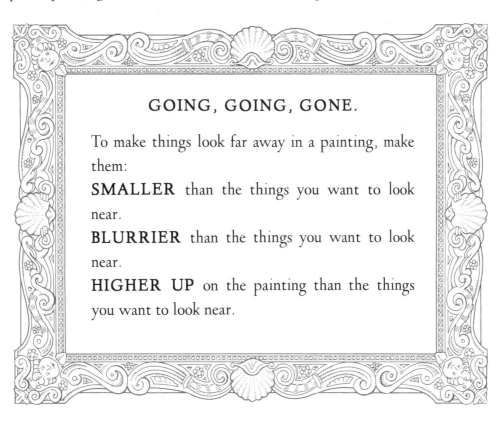

**GOING, GOING, GONE.**

To make things look far away in a painting, make them:

**SMALLER** than the things you want to look near.

**BLURRIER** than the things you want to look near.

**HIGHER UP** on the painting than the things you want to look near.

## 1. SMALLER

Which did the artist paint smaller? (check one):

_____ the church          _____ the tree to the boy's left

## 2. BLURRIER

Which did the artist paint blurrier? (check one):

_____ the mountains        _____ the train

## 3. HIGHER UP

Which did the artist paint higher up on the painting? (check one):

_____ the roundhouse       _____ the tree stumps

Which one in each pair of answers looks furthest away?
Circle your guess in each pair.

## Activity: Panorama Diorama

A **PANORAMA** is a view as far as your eyes can see of the world around you. It can cover miles and miles and miles, like the painting *The Lackawanna Valley*. A **DIORAMA** is an art project that you can make at home. It is the re-creation of a scene, such as a giant, beautiful panorama, inside a shoe box. By placing little trees, mountains, and other things that you cut from paper and glue into the shoe box, you can create the look of a deep, enormous space.

You will need:

an empty shoe box
construction paper
glue
crayons, paints, or markers
scissors

Think of your favorite landscape: maybe it is the mountains in winter, a valley on a sunny spring day, or the beach and ocean at sunrise. Picture it in your mind.

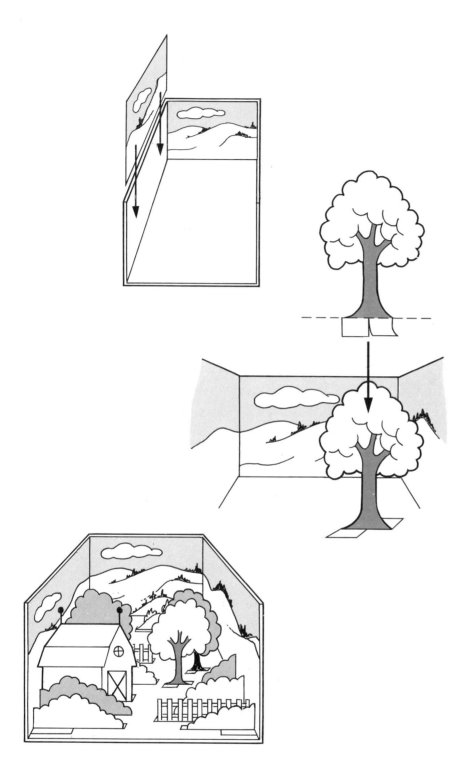

Cut one end out of a shoebox. Measure the sides and the other end of the box and cut out pieces of paper to match those sizes.

This is your background. Draw and paint those pieces with the faraway scene in your landscape. Is there a lot of sky? mountains? a sunset? Will it be clear and detailed or a bit blurry?

Now paste those pieces of paper inside the shoebox onto the sides and back.

For things that are closer in your landscape, you can draw them on paper or use cut-outs from magazines. When you cut out their shapes, include an extra inch of paper on the bottom of each. Fold this paper tab back to create a stand and glue it to the shoebox floor so the shape stands by itself. You can have many layers to your landscape, with things at different distances from one another. What will be closest and what will be farthest away? What will be bigger and what will be smaller? Experiment with the three art tricks you just learned on your adventure in the Lackawanna Valley.

# Adventure Number 25

## 2–D or Not 2–D, That Is the Question.

Georges Braque. (French, 1882–1963) *Still Life: Le Jour.* 1929

Everything in this world has a shape—a school bus, a shoe, a mountain, and a house. Draw a house on a separate piece of paper.

Your drawing probably shows the front of a house, with a door and some windows, and maybe a roof and a chimney.

But isn't there more to a house than its front? What about the sides of the house, the back, the roof from the top, the inside? It's IMPOSSIBLE in one picture to draw the ENTIRE house because:

1) Your eyes can't see all the different parts at one time.
   You can only look at and draw one view at a time.

2) A piece of paper is flat. When something is flat, it is TWO-DIMENSIONAL or 2-D. It has only:

**LENGTH**  **WIDTH**

Something that's two-dimensional is nothing that you can hug or put your hand around.

These things are two-dimensional: a postcard, a stamp, a dollar bill.

Can you list two more things that are two-dimensional?

1._____     2._____

The artist Georges Braque wanted to be able to show several different views of one thing in a picture. He wanted to show the front, back, inside, and outside of an object at the same time, all on one painting surface. What do you call something that has LENGTH, WIDTH, and DEPTH? Look in the Magic Picture Frame for an answer that you can really grasp.

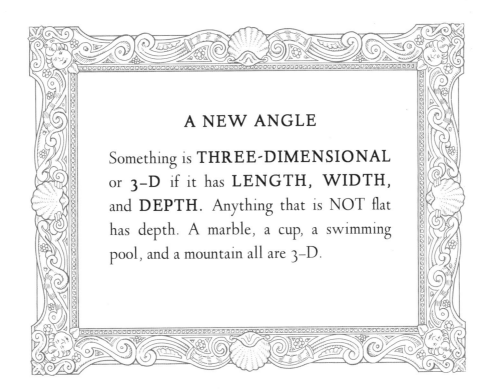

### A NEW ANGLE

Something is **THREE-DIMENSIONAL** or **3-D** if it has **LENGTH, WIDTH, and DEPTH.** Anything that is NOT flat has depth. A marble, a cup, a swimming pool, and a mountain all are 3-D.

List four other **THREE-DIMENSIONAL** things:

1. _____ 2. _____ 3. _____ 4. _____

Now look at the painting on page 104. It is a **STILL LIFE**, which is a grouping of objects such as books or flowers, dishes, or fruit. What objects did Braque include in his still life? **A**₁ Name six.

1. _____ 2. _____ 3. _____ 4. _____ 5. _____ 6. _____

Here is a painting of what a guitar looks like.

Auguste Renoir. *Young Spanish Woman with a Guitar.* 1898

Now find a guitar in Braque's painting. Does it look the same? No. Not only is the guitar in Braque's painting a funny shape with strange curves and bulges, but you can also see many different views of the guitar at the same time. You see the front of it and the two sides of the guitar in his painting. In real life, your eye could never see both sides and the front of the guitar at one time.

Now look at the table. How many different parts of it did the artist show you all at once? **A**₂ (Circle all that you can see in the painting)

one side          the top          an open drawer          the back          table legs
the feet of the table

Imagine that there really is a table that looks just like this. What would happen to all the things resting on the table top?

**CRASH!!!!!**

# Activity: Don't Be a Square

On the right is a funny looking shape. Because it is on a page of a book, it is only **two-dimensional**. However, when you copy the shape onto a piece of cardboard and follow some simple instructions, you can turn it into a fancy, **three-dimensional** box. Read how.

1) Trace the whole picture with a pencil, including the dotted lines and numbers, onto a piece of white paper.

2) Cut it out, but cut only where you see a SOLID line. Do not cut on the dotted lines. Glue it onto a piece of white poster board or cardboard. Cut the cardboard shape exactly where the paper has been cut.

3) Carefully bend inward on all the dotted lines. Make nice creases. Bending lines over a ruler can help.

4) On the OUTSIDE of #1 put a little glue. Fold the box so #1 is glued to the INSIDE of #2.

5) Do the same with the OUTSIDE of #3, folding it inward and gluing it to the INSIDE of #2.

6) Put a little glue on the INSIDE of #4. Fold it over and tuck it in to make one end of the box.

7) Do the same with the other end of the box.

8) Decorate the box with paints, markers, or crayons. Use your special 3-D box to hold paper clips, coins, or a secret treasure.

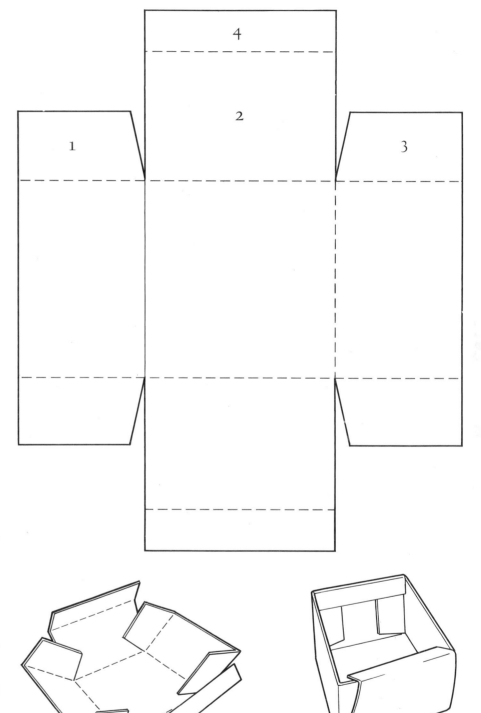

# If You Visit The National Gallery of Art or Another Museum

The National Gallery of Art is an enormous art museum. There is too much to see in one visit, so take your time and look at just a few things. You can get a map at the Information Desks to help you decide what to see. You will also see some men and women in uniforms throughout the building. These people are guards. It is their job to help you with directions and to make sure you understand all the rules. Be sure to say hello to them.

Do you know the different rules at the National Gallery of Art and at most other art museums?
1) You cannot touch any of the art because the oils on your fingertips (even though your hands look clean) will make the work of art dirty. If everyone touched, the art would be ruined, and no one would be able to enjoy it. We want it to last as long as possible.
2) You cannot run through the museum because we don't want you or the art to get hurt.
3) You cannot shout or be very loud; other people are trying to enjoy their visit too.
These three rules are easy to follow and will help everyone have a fun and safe visit.

The activities in this book will give you some great ideas for things to do when looking at art. You might even want to bring the book along on your visit to the National Gallery to look for the paintings that are mentioned. Make a game of trying to find them in the museum. Sometimes a painting that you are looking for will not be hanging: it may be that it is being cleaned or is on loan to another museum for a special exhibition.

Below are questions that you can ask yourself in front of ANY work of art.
1) HOW did the artist make the work of art? What materials were used? Do you think it took a long or short time to make? Why?
2) WHY do you think the artist made the work of art? What was he or she thinking or trying to do?
3) Pretend that you could step inside the work of art and be a part of it. What would you see? hear? smell? feel? do?
4) If you gave the work of art a title, what would it be, and why?
5) What COLORS can you find? Are there several shades or tints of any one color? What SHAPES can you find? Are there any shapes repeated in the work of art? Are there thick or thin LINES? straight or curvy lines?
6) If you are in a room with many works of art, decide which ones you would want in

| | |
|---|---|
| your bedroom | your parent's bedroom |
| the living room | the attic or basement where it can be hidden if you don't like it |

# The Answer Page

ADVENTURE NUMBER 1:

1. Yes, every color has many shades and tints. Experiment with your crayons, paints, or markers.

ADVENTURE NUMBER 2:

1. The style of their clothes; their hairstyle.
2. It was very fashionable long ago in America for men to "silver" their hair with powder or to wear wigs.
3. A print, such as the dollar bill, is made by first scratching a picture onto a flat piece of metal with a sharp tool. When ink is put on top of the metal, it flows into the scratches. The rest of the ink is wiped away, so that when the metal plate is pressed hard onto a piece of clean paper, only the ink from lines of the picture is transferred onto the paper. Many prints can be made from this same piece of metal by putting ink on it again and again.

ADVENTURE NUMBER 4:

1. A mobile is a work of art that moves.
2. aluminum (metal)
3. They look like triangles with rounded corners and they hang from top to bottom.
4. They are shaped like wedges, a bit like birds flying, and they hang flat.
5. slowly
6. smoothly

ADVENTURE NUMBER 5:

1.

ADVENTURE NUMBER 6:

1. sight, sound, taste, touch, smell
2. See the completed word puzzle.

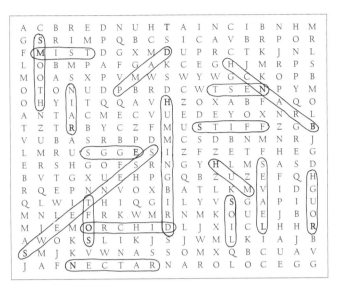

ADVENTURE NUMBER 7:

1. Napoleon was up all night working.

ADVENTURE NUMBER 8:

1. On the side of the stage, out of the audience's view.
2. Pissarro painted this from a window in his room high up in the Grand Hotel de Russie, Paris.

ADVENTURE NUMBER 9:

1. 1) Row, row, row        2) Merrily, merrily, merrily

ADVENTURE NUMBER 10:

1. 80 pounds        2. 40 pounds        3. 30 pounds
4. Sheet music, pipe, book, flute

ADVENTURE NUMBER 11:

1. their shells
2. their horns
3. their scent glands
4. It is shaped like a person's upper body, with the top wide enough to protect the chest and shoulders.

ADVENTURE NUMBER 12:

1. black, white, blue-gray, soft pink

ADVENTURE NUMBER 13:

1.

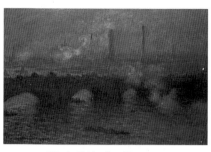

Waterloo Bridge, Gray Day. 1903

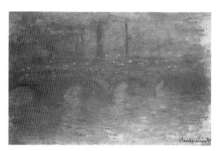

Waterloo Bridge, London, at Dusk. 1904

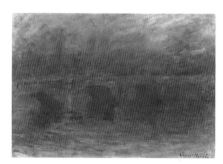

Waterloo Bridge, London, at Sunset. 1904

ADVENTURE NUMBER 14:

1. a boat hook, a man reaching overboard

ADVENTURE NUMBER 16:

1. red, blue, yellow, green, black, orange

ADVENTURE NUMBER 17:

1. a triangle, a circle
2. five racers
3. at least eight wheels

ADVENTURE NUMBER 19:

1.  Gloucester
2.  1) the small, choppy waves
    2) the tilt of the boat in the water
    3) the sail of the boat filled with air
    4) the sail of the boat in the distance
    5) the boys leaning back to balance the boat
    6) the water spray kicked up by the boat
3.  1) inside part of the sail
    2) the boys' shoulders
    3) the tops of their hats, especially the skipper's
    4) the water immediately surrounding the boat
4.  Shadows appear on the inside of the sail; on the deck of the boat; on the water surrounding the boat.
5.  C

ADVENTURE NUMBER 20:

1. metal
2. 1) Stella thought of the idea 2) Stella made drawings of the idea and designed the shapes 3) The metal was cut into shapes by metal workers 4) He painted the metal shapes 5) The shapes were put together according to his drawings

ADVENTURE NUMBER 21:

1. Dove=Peace; Lion=Courage; Bee=Busyness; Dog=Faithfulness; Owl=Wisdom

ADVENTURE NUMBER 23:

1. Wine jug=wine bottle; Knickers=pants; violin, flute=stereo; pointed shoe=shoe; ruffled collar=shirt collar
2. Jan Steen is on the left side of the painting, sitting behind the table and leaning over.

ADVENTURE NUMBER 25:

1. Pipe, apples, knife, table, jug, guitar, newspaper
2. One side, the top, an open drawer, and table legs

# Glossary

BALANCE—an even distribution of weight.

CANVAS—a heavy fabric that artists paint on.

COLLAGE—a composition created by combining various materials. Collage can be used in combination with other art techniques.

COMPOSITION—the arrangement or placement of things in a work of art.

DEPTH—the third dimension, after height and width.

DIAGONAL—having a slanted direction.

DIORAMA—the artistic recreation of a scene inside a little box.

EASEL—a frame or stand that holds the picture the artist works on.

ENGRAVING—a print made by cutting a design into a metal plate with a pointed tool. Ink is rubbed into the design and then wiped off the surface. Paper is placed on top of the plate and both are run through a heavy press so that the picture is transferred to the paper.

IMPRESSIONISTS—artists in the late 1800s who painted out of doors and tried to capture the changing effects of sunlight and color.

LANDSCAPE—a picture of a place in the outdoors.

LENGTH—the measurement of how long something is.

MEDIUM—the material that holds together the pigments of a paint.

MOBILE—a work of art that moves.

MUSEUM—a place where a collection of similar things is gathered, kept, cared for, and displayed.

OIL PAINT—paint made from mixing pigment with oil.

OVAL—egg-shape.

PANORAMA—an extremely wide view of the world.

PATTERN—a design that is repeated over and over again.

PIGMENT—any substance, usually powdered, that is used as coloring. It can be mixed with water, egg yolk, or oil to make paint.

PORTRAIT—a picture of a person.

PRINT—a picture or design reproduced, usually on paper and often in numerous copies, from a wood block, metal plate, or stone slab that has been carved into and covered with ink or paint.

SELF-PORTRAIT—a picture of the artist.

SERIES—a group of related works of art.

SHADE—a color with black added to it.

STILL LIFE—a painting of a group of objects.

STYLE—the way something is painted; an artist's individual technique.

SUBJECT—the main thing, person, or event that the artist is making a work of art about.

SYMBOL—a picture that stands for an idea.

TEMPERA PAINT—paint made from mixing powdered pigment with egg yolk.

TEXTURE—the way something looks and feels; smooth, bumpy, rough, sticky.

THREE-DIMENSIONAL—something that has length, width, and depth; in other words, not flat.

TINT—color with white added to it.

TWO-DIMENSIONAL—something that has only length and width.

WIDTH—the measurement of how wide something is.

# Picture Credits

Introduction:

Claude Monet
*The Bridge at Argenteuil*, 1874
Collection of Mr. and Mrs. Paul Mellon

Antonio Rossellino
*The Young Saint John the Baptist*, c. 1470
Samuel H. Kress Collection

Peter Paul Rubens
*Lion*, c. 1612–13
Ailsa Mellon Bruce Fund

ADVENTURE NUMBER 1:

Henri Rousseau
*Tropical Forest with Monkeys*, 1910
John Hay Whitney Collection

ADVENTURE NUMBER 2:

Gilbert Stuart
*George Washington (Athenaeum portrait)*, c. 1821
Gift of Thomas Jefferson Coolidge IV in memory of his great-grandfather, Thomas Jefferson Coolidge, his grandfather, Thomas Jefferson Coolidge II, and his father, Thomas Jefferson Coolidge III

Stuart, *John Adams*, c. 1821
Ailsa Mellon Bruce Fund

Stuart, *Thomas Jefferson*, c. 1821
Gift of Thomas Jefferson Coolidge IV in memory of his great-grandfather, Thomas Jefferson Coolidge, his grandfather, Thomas Jefferson Coolidge II, and his father, Thomas Jefferson Coolidge III

Stuart, *James Madison*, c. 1821
Ailsa Mellon Bruce Fund

Stuart, *James Monroe*, c. 1817
Ailsa Mellon Bruce Fund

ADVENTURE NUMBER 3:

Auguste Renoir
*A Girl with a Watering Can*, 1876
Chester Dale Collection

Claude Monet
*Woman with a Parasol—Madame Monet and Her Son*, 1875
Collection of Mr. and Mrs. Paul Mellon

Berthe Morisot
*The Mother and Sister of the Artist*, 1869/1870
Chester Dale Collection

ADVENTURE NUMBER 4:

Alexander Calder
*Untitled*, 1976
Gift of the Collectors Committee

Calders listed below are gifts from Mrs. Paul Mellon in Honor of the Fiftieth Anniversary of the National Gallery of Art:

Calder: *La Vache*, 1970; *Black Camel with Blue Head and Red Tongue*, 1971

ADVENTURE NUMBER 5:

Nicolas Poussin
*The Assumption of the Virgin*, c. 1626
Ailsa Mellon Bruce Fund

Antoine Watteau
*Italian Comedians*, probably 1720
Samuel H. Kress Collection

ADVENTURE NUMBER 6:

Martin Johnson Heade
*Cattleya Orchid and Three Brazilian Hummingbirds*, 1871
Gift of the Morris and Gwendolyn Cafritz Foundation

ADVENTURE NUMBER 7:

Jacques-Louis David
*Napoleon in His Study*, 1812
Samuel H. Kress Collection

ADVENTURE NUMBER 8:

Edgar Degas
*Dancers at the Old Opera House*, c. 1877
Ailsa Mellon Bruce Collection

Camille Pissarro
*Boulevard des Italiens, Morning, Sunlight*, 1897
Chester Dale Collection

ADVENTURE NUMBER 9:

Gustave Caillebotte
*Skiffs*, 1877
Collection of Mr. and Mrs. Paul Mellon

Henri Matisse
*Pianist and Checker Players*, 1924
Collection of Mr. and Mrs. Paul Mellon

ADVENTURE NUMBER 10:

William Michael Harnett
*My Gems*, 1888
Gift of the Avalon Foundation

ADVENTURE NUMBER 11:

Andrea del Castagno
*The Youthful David*, c. 1450
Widener Collection

ADVENTURE NUMBER 12:

Jackson Pollock
*Number 1, 1950 (Lavender Mist)*, 1950
Ailsa Mellon Bruce Fund

ADVENTURE NUMBER 13:

Claude Monet
*Waterloo Bridge, Gray Day*, 1903
Chester Dale Collection

Monet, *Waterloo Bridge, London, at Dusk*, 1904
Collection of Mr. and Mrs. Paul Mellon

Monet, *Waterloo Bridge, London, at Sunset*, 1904
Collection of Mr. and Mrs. Paul Mellon

ADVENTURE NUMBER 14:

John Singleton Copley
*Watson and the Shark*, 1778
Ferdinand Lammot Belin Fund

Peter Paul Rubens
*Daniel in the Lions' Den*, c. 1613/1615
Ailsa Mellon Bruce Fund

ADVENTURE NUMBER 15:

James Jacques Joseph Tissot
*Hide and Seek*, c. 1877
Chester Dale Fund

Chuck Close
*Fanny/Fingerpainting*, 1985
Gift of Lila Acheson Wallace

ADVENTURE NUMBER 16:

Wassily Kandinsky
*Improvisation 31 (Sea Battle)*, 1913
Ailsa Mellon Bruce Fund

Jean-Honoré Fragonard
*Blindman's Bluff (detail)*, probably c. 1765
Samuel H. Kress Collection

Jean-Honoré Fragonard
*The Swing (detail)*, probably c. 1765
Samuel H. Kress Collection

Pablo Picasso
*The Tragedy*, 1903
Chester Dale Collection

ADVENTURE NUMBER 17:

Paul Cézanne
*Houses in Provence*, c. 1880
Collection of Mr. and Mrs. Paul Mellon

Pablo Picasso
*Madame Picasso*, 1923
Chester Dale Collection

Lyonel Feininger
*The Bicycle Race*, 1912
Collection of Mr. and Mrs. Paul Mellon

ADVENTURE NUMBER 18:

Robert Henri
*Snow in New York*, 1902
Chester Dale Collection

André Derain
*Mountains at Collioure*, 1905
John Hay Whitney Collection

ADVENTURE NUMBER 19:

Winslow Homer
*Breezing Up (A Fair Wind)*, 1876
Gift of the W. L. and May T. Mellon Foundation

Rembrandt van Rijn
*The Mill*, 1645/1648
Widener Collection

ADVENTURE NUMBER 20:

Frank Stella
*Jarama II*, 1982
Gift of Lila Acheson Wallace

ADVENTURE NUMBER 21:

Rogier van der Weyden
*Saint George and the Dragon*, c. 1432/1435
Ailsa Mellon Bruce Fund

ADVENTURE NUMBER 22:

George Catlin
*The White Cloud, Head Chief of the Iowas*, 1844/1845
Paul Mellon Collection

Catlin, *Buffalo Lancing in the Snow Drifts—Sioux*, 1861/1869
Paul Mellon Collection

ADVENTURE NUMBER 23:

Jan Steen
*The Dancing Couple*, 1663
Widener Collection

After Lucas van Leyden
*The Card Players*, probably c. 1550/1599
Samuel H. Kress Collection

Linton Park
*Flax Scutching Bee*, 1885
Gift of Edgar William and Bernice Chrysler Garbisch

ADVENTURE NUMBER 24:

George Inness
*The Lackawanna Valley*, 1855
Gift of Mrs. Huttleston Rogers

ADVENTURE NUMBER 25:

Georges Braque
*Still Life: Le Jour*, 1929
Chester Dale Collection

The photograph of the front of the West Building of the National Gallery on page 6 is by Dennis Brack.